Discounted Cash Flow

second edition

Discounted Cash Flow

second edition

M. G. Wright, BCom, ACCA, FCIS
School of Management Studies, The Polytechnic of Central London

McGRAW-HILL Book Company (UK) Limited

London · New York · St Louis · San Francisco · Auckland
Bogotá · Guatemala · Hamburg · Johannesburg · Lisbon
Madrid · Mexico · Montreal · New Delhi · Panama · Paris
San Juan · São Paulo · Singapore · Sydney · Tokyo · Toronto

Published by
McGRAW-HILL Book Company (UK) Limited
MAIDENHEAD · BERKSHIRE · ENGLAND

07 084425 9

45678 CD & B 81079

PRINTED IN GREAT BRITAIN

To my parents

Preface

In the six years since this book was first published, discounted cash flow has become a more widely accepted technique for capital investment appraisal. While there has been an intellectual acceptance of the technique it is questionable whether its practical application is as widespread as is sometimes thought. There is still an urgent demand for managers to understand the way DCF can assist in the decision-making process and avoid some of the 'mystique' which surrounds the subject in some quarters. At the same time, the major changes that are taking place in the tax structure in the United Kingdom require some reappraisal of the implications of taxation for cash flows.

The lack of acceptance of the technique by some managers may rest on the belief that it is derived from economic theory and can only be really mastered by those with an understanding of higher mathematics. The purpose of this book is to show the underlying simplicity of the technique and to demonstrate its application to typical real life situations. Even where the more sophisticated forms of DCF are used, including the use of the computer, the manager should be able to understand the implications for the rate of return of the factors used and to interpret the solution.

DCF involves greater discipline in forecasting techniques, since its use will usually involve placing definite values on more aspects of the project than heretofore. When allied to the use of post-audit techniques, this may provide secondary benefits through raising the quality of forecasting and providing it with a greater degree of precision.

One cannot overemphasize that DCF is only a technique and is not a substitute for proper management decision taking. Prominence has been given in the text to the relationship between corporate and financial planning and the capital investment decision in order that the role of DCF is made quite clear. Its real merits must be kept in proper perspective and its subordination to long-term planning appreciated if it is to play a really meaningful role.

Improving the rate of profitability on capital invested is just as important to the economic well being of any country as increasing the volume of capital invested. Unprofitable investments and those showing a low rate of return must be avoided as far as possible, both from the point of view of the individual firm and of the country as a whole. DCF has a part to play in investment decision taking, and it is hoped that this book will contribute to a fuller understanding and use of the technique for this purpose. It is not an answer to all problems, but it is an analytical tool that can be of great benefit to management.

My grateful thanks are due to my wife, Kathleen, for her forbearance and help. I am indebted also to International Computers Limited for their permission to reproduce material from their PROP programme.

M. G. WRIGHT

Contents

List of Figures

List of Tables

1 Capital Investment Appraisal and Profitability

As its title implies, this book is concerned with the meaning and use of discounted cash flow (DCF) and how management can use the technique. It would, however, be unrealistic to discuss the technique without first examining how it fits in to the general management processes, and, in particular, the crucial role of funds allocation in determining the level of profitability. The present vogue for 'scientific' management techniques endows them with decision-making qualities which quite frequently they do not possess. This applies to DCF and leads to a wrong emphasis being given to management decisions and the use of the technique and dissatisfaction with the result. It is therefore essential at the outset to examine the general and financial management planning and control areas as they affect investment decisions.

Profitability and Growth

The measurement and control of profitability in commercially orientated organizations forms one of the principle objectives of the financial function. While the word *profit* is sometimes considered dirty, long-term profitability is the only criterion that should be used to measure the efficiency of the management team.

The level of profitability achieved has a decisive influence upon growth prospects. A company with a low level of profitability will generate little profit compared with similar businesses, and since it is only out of such profits that provision can be made for future growth and the payment of dividends, these will both be restricted. Low profitability, by reducing the potential return to shareholders, limits the possibility of raising fresh shareholder's funds, and, by reducing the cover for debt service, limits the use of borrowing as a source of finance. Both limitations drastically affect the expansion prospects of any business and induce a state of stagnation.

The business with a high level of profitability, on the other hand, generates a large flow of funds out of which it can provide for both funding new expansion and an increasing return to the shareholders. It will be an attractive

1

investment for the suppliers of both equity and borrowed funds which will enable it to attract any additional funds quite easily.

Just as the level of profitability is of vital importance to the financial health of a business, so it is of importance to the health of a national economy. National policy should be to encourage the highest level of profitability on the resources employed for business activities, as distinct from social or military uses. No advanced country today can avoid the problem of providing at least some social services for at least some sections of the community, and of providing for internal and external security. Inevitably a proportion of a country's resources will be absorbed by such requirements. The remaining resources will have to provide the means of financing such expenditures, and this will be critically affected by the level of return earned on those resources devoted to commercial and industrial purposes.

QUALITY OF INVESTMENT

Commentators and politicians in the United Kingdom have continually urged industrialists to invest ever greater amounts in productive facilities since the Second World War. In this concentration upon the *volume* of investment, the *quality* of investment has sometimes been lost to sight. Artifically making projects profitable through tax incentives and grants is no substitute for a situation which is conducive to fundamentally sound, i.e., profitable, investments.

If £1 million is invested in a sophisticated plant to make, say, shoes, and that plant does nothing more than break even, then the investment of that money and the underlying resources used contribute nothing to the resources of the firm or the country. However, a similar investment that yields a profit before tax of 20 per cent on the capital invested contributes to corporate growth, and through taxation and the increase in real resources contributes to the national well being. There is therefore no conflict between the national interest and that of the firm. Indeed, the former will be reinforced if it is based upon a large number of profitable companies. This will be true irrespective of the political system under which the country functions.

LONG-TERM NATURE OF INVESTMENT DECISIONS

Management's decisions committing the funds of a business to specific uses is at the heart of the factors which determine profitability. The management which is able to generate innovative ideas and from these select projects which will provide a high rate of return with a high probability of success will build up a profitable firm, whereas the firm with few prospects for investment giving a worthwhile return, or whose selection of projects is poor, will, in general, tend to be one with a low level of profitability.

The investment of funds in a project locks up those funds in that use for a long period of time. Investment in a highly automated plant cannot be reversed quickly. The funds will remain there until they are recouped

2

through earning profits and the related depreciation, or the assets are scrapped. It is this long-term characteristic that distinguishes investment from other business decisions. Setting the wrong stock levels or allowing credit periods to be extended are mistakes that can be remedied reasonably quickly by management. The timescale of such corrections is short term, being determined solely by factors such as the length of time it takes to absorb or sell surplus stock, or to collect debtor's accounts. The timespan for correcting wrong investment decisions will, however, be the normal working life of the plant unless the firm decides to write off the funds as having been lost.

It is not only funds invested in *fixed* assets that will be locked up by the wrong investment decisions. The employment of fixed assets will, in many cases, need to be backed up by an investment in stocks and work in progress and debtors. The investment decision, therefore, influences the totality of funds employed and the way in which they are allocated to particular uses.

Given that each firm has in each year a finite sum of funds available to finance new investment, then each commitment of funds to an unprofitable investment decreases the amount available for other, perhaps profitable, investments. Moreover, the diminution of profits due to such unprofitable investment, by reducing or restricting the amount of funds available in future years, limits investment in the future. The way in which the business allocates the resources at its disposal will, therefore, have a far-reaching effect on its profitability as a whole. The decision processes by which funds are allocated and the criteria used for selection of projects require definition, together with management's role at each stage.

Allocation a Two-Stage Process

Today, it is widely recognized, if not practised, that the allocation of funds requires something more than a simple selection process using the test of profitability. This does not mean that relative profitability does not have a vital role to play in the system of funds allocation. What it does recognize is that this selection should not be the only criterion. One of top management's vital roles is to ensure the long-term viability of the business and, as such, should be seeking to maximize long-term rather than short-term profitability. The initiation of investment proposals on the other hand, often comes from lower levels of management who are more concerned with immediate profitability and who frequently identify their personal objectives with the section of the business that they control.

The requirement for long-term profitability indicates that there should, in effect, be a two-level allocation of funds:

1. *Primary Allocation.* The primary allocation should be made at board of director or equivalent level, in order to ensure that there is the right

3

balance of resources required to achieve the long-term goals of the organization.

2. *Project Selection.* Within the strategic allocation above, this stage comprises the normal process of formulating new investment proposals, appraisal by profitability criteria, and their approval by management.

This splitting of the process of allocating funds is not a pedantic exercise, but a division of function that is fundamental in importance. Too often British industry blurrs or fails to take note of this distinction. The function of the board is to set out the general policy and direction of the business, and if it carries out this function adequately then it cannot really avoid making the strategic allocation of funds required to achieve the corporate goals.

This process can perhaps be compared with the function of the chiefs of staff of the armed forces in war time. They set out the general objectives to be pursued in each theatre of operations, and allocate the resources at their disposal in such a way as to maximize the possibility of bringing the war to a successful conclusion. Within the resources allocated to him each theatre commander attempts to formulate operations to achieve the objectives his chiefs of staff have set for him, and obtain approval for such operations to be mounted. This allocation of resources and approval of individual operations will be the method by which the chiefs of staff ensure that the war effort as a whole pursues the objectives laid down, and that each theatre commander does not fight his own particular war without regard to the balance of the war effort as a whole. Although there will be consultations and discussions at all levels of command, this cohesion will be achieved principally by policy making and resource allocation at the top.

Just as in the services policy decisions cannot be left to subordinate commanders, so, in the business world, they should not be left to line management. Policy making should always be under the control and direction of the board of directors who should be responsible for giving the business its sense of purpose and stimulus.

CORPORATE STRATEGY

This policy making process is today usually formalized under some such title as *corporate strategy* or *long-range planning*. It is, in fact, the starting point for all decision making in an organization. It comprises the definition of the objectives of the business, how they are to be achieved, and the resources that will be required.

The process of formulating the corporate strategy can be summarized as follows:

1. *Definition of objectives.* It can be argued that all commercially orientated organizations have the same basic objective—to make a profit. Other objectives such as 'to be the technological leaders in the in-

4

dustry', or 'to achieve a stated market share', will, if they lead to unprofitable operations, be revised. They are, in effect, subject to the test of profitability. What is an *acceptable* level of profit will be defined in terms of return on capital employed and the related long-term return to shareholders. The measurement of this acceptable level of profit requires managerial decisions about:

(*a*) The mix of funds to be used (essentially the balance between borrowing and ordinary shareholder's funds).*

(*b*) The volume of funds to be employed.

(*c*) The dividend policy (the higher the proportion of profits paid out, the higher is likely to be the share price and, therefore, the overall return to shareholders).

2. *The strategy.* Having defined the level of profit that must be achieved to make the company viable in the long term, to the extent of offering an adequate return to shareholders, management must then make decisions about *how* it is going to achieve the desired levels of profits. To do this, it will make an appraisal of the strengths and weaknesses of the company so that it has an adequate view of why the business has been successful in the past and what deficiencies exist that obstruct better performance. There must also be an appraisal of the environment within which the business operates and the likely direction and extent of technological and social changes. Decisions must then be made about what the business should do if it is to take advantage of the opportunities that may be presented by such changes. At the end of the process, decisions will have been made about:

(*a*) Product development.

(*b*) Physical resources, e.g., plant and equipment, buildings, etc., that will be required.

(*c*) Human resources in terms of numbers and skills.

(*d*) Marketing and other functional policies.

(*e*) Organizational structure.

(*f*) Financial resources.

It can be seen that the above process has outlined in broad terms the direction and volume of new investment over the planning period. It has set the framework within which the capital budgeting process must operate and will have defined target or acceptable levels of profitability for use in the appraisal process.

OTHER CONSIDERATIONS IN PROJECT APPRAISAL

Apart from the requirements of the corporate strategy there are other considerations which may have to be taken into account when considering the capital budget. For example, the high profitability projects may all be

* See Gearing on page 134.

5

ones where there are little, if any, profits in the early years, but large ones in later years. If adopted, this might result in the company reporting sharply reduced profits during those early years with adverse effects for the company, e.g., through a reduced share price, and for shareholders who wish to sell during that period. Management would have to make a choice between a mix of new investments which gave a smoother pattern of profits year by year or that which gave the highest level of profitability but with uneven earnings.

Other factors will include that of uncertainty and risk. This will be dealt with in greater depth later on, but they are factors which clearly enter into management's considerations.

The primary allocation of funds has been stressed at some length. And not without reason. In most businesses, line managers originate investment proposals. If the board then merely allocates the available resources by ranking such proposals in order of profitability, the resulting disposition of funds may not be in accordance with the requirements of the corporate strategy. Line managers may not be fully informed of the corporate strategy of the business that they serve or be in a position to weigh up the relative merits of the proposals as they affect the business as a whole. Their horizon tends to be restricted by the immediate environment within which they work, and this may only be a small segment of the business, and since they are competing with each other for a limited amount of funds their judgement may be impaired by this fact. The corporate strategy is essential to get all the parts of the business working together towards the common objective.

MINIMUM PROFITABILITY CRITERION

Figure 1.1 shows the flow of funds in a business. The funds required to finance its long-term growth are derived from (a) the owners, in the company structure this comprises ordinary and preferred shareholders' funds including undistributed reserves; (b) borrowed funds comprising mortgages, debentures, and secured and unsecured loans. Each year the new funds available will be drawn from one or both of these sources together with the undistributed profit for the year and depreciation. These funds form the 'pool' of funds that is available for investment.

This pool has a cost. This is clearly seen in the case of borrowing where interest has to be paid. The original funds invested by shareholders and the profits of one sort or another which they have allowed to remain in the business also have a cost. The measurement of this cost is dealt with on page 136. At this stage, it is enough to say that the shareholders could earn a return on those funds if they were invested in uses other than in the company under discussion.

It can be seen that the capital investment decision stands at the interface between the acquisition of the various sources of funds and their being committed to specific uses. One aim of that decision area should be to ensure

6

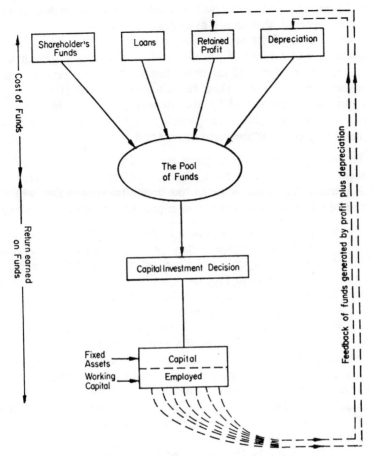

Figure 1.1. The flow of funds

that the uses to which management puts the pool of funds earns at least as much as the cost of those funds to the pool. If the average cost of funds to the pool is 10 per cent after tax and the company puts the funds to work where it only earn 8 per cent, the prospects for that company and its shareholders are, to say the least, very bleak. The judgements made about the minimum level of profitability for projects must be based upon earning more than the cost of the pool of funds.

Selection of Projects

Once the primary allocation of funds has been completed the business must have some method of selecting the projects in which it will invest the funds that it has available, or will raise from outside sources. It is this stage in the evaluation of capital investments with which this book is primarily con-

7

cerned. In particular, the book will be dealing with one method of capital investment appraisal, that known as *discounted cash flow*.

The object of any system of project selection is to be able to compare the profitability of a series of possible uses of funds. Each project will require the use of a volume of the firm's funds for varying periods, and will also provide for the return of those funds together with an element of profit. The appraisal system should be able to take both these factors and, by comparing them, calculate a comparable rate of return. This will enable investment projects to be measured against two criteria:

1. To ensure that out of any given series of investment proposals, only those projects that give the highest rates of return are selected.
2. To ensure that investments are not made in projects that will give a rate of return less than the cost of capital employed in the business.

Few businesses will have available a large enough volume of funds to be able to invest in all the projects it may have in the pipeline. Management must therefore have at its command a method of applying the above criteria to each investment proposal. To cover the first of these criteria, the method used must be able to rank projects in order of profitability so that the relative desirability of each project can be readily seen.

The second of the criteria requires a comparison between the return that can be earned on the project and the cost of the funds to the business. Although each business may have an overall limit to the amount of funds available, that limit may be wide enough to allow the selection of so many projects that some of them have a rate of return that is lower than the cost of capital to the business. Where this arises, management must then set a 'cut-off' or criterion rate of return that will be a minimum acceptable rate of return for any project.

This cut-off rate will be closely related to the cost of capital but may be adjusted for a number of factors, including an allowance for the uncertainty embodied in the estimated rates of return, and for the investment of some funds in projects that have no rate of return. Where the return on a project does not meet the cut-off rate, then management must decide whether it will carry the excess funds forward until more profitable projects become available, or whether some of the funds employed in the business should be repaid, either to the people who have loaned money to the business or to the owners of the business.

A note was made in the previous paragraph that some investment projects may have no rate of return and not be subject to the two criteria mentioned. Certain money may have to be invested in order that the business can continue to be carried on, without affecting the level of profits at all. For example, the local authority may require modernization of toilet facilities, or the provision of adequate car-parking facilities for the firm's employees. Such investments must be made without recourse to the criteria mentioned above. Similarly, some projects, such as the provision of recreational and canteen facilities, may be impossible of assessment by rate of return criteria, but, for policy reasons formulated by management, may still be considered as appropriate uses of the funds of the business.

TYPES OF PROBLEM

The investment of funds within the business will present management with a number of different types of problem each requiring a different approach for its solution. These types may be broadly classified as in Table 1.1.

TABLE 1.1. *Types of Investment Problems*

1. *Expansion*	Whether to build and equip a new factory or expand other facilities	The investment is the amount that will be locked up by such an expansion, which will be measured against the additional profits that are expected to flow from such an expansion
2. *Replacement and moderniza-tion*	Replacement of existing plant by more efficient plant	The return on this investment will be the savings in costs that are expected to flow from the use of more efficient plant
3. *Choice problems*	In 1 and 2 above there may be more than one way of achieving the desired result. Management must be able to choose the most profitable alternative	Alternative methods must be ranked in order of profitability in order to select that which shows the highest rate of return
4. *Lease or buy*	Whether to lease or buy the equipment. This is a specialized aspect of choice problems	When a project is approved there can be a further level of analysis. Purchase involves the commitment of funds, and this can be compared with the savings in rental, etc., that would ensue
5. *Financing problems*	Whether to redeem loans or Preference shares and replace with funds with a lower cost, and choice among alternative methods of financing	The refunding operation will involve costs and, probably, a premium on the funds redeemed. These costs are compared with the interest, etc., saved as a result of the operation

Evaluation of Investment Problems

The basic principle underlying all the types of problem outlined above is that the net return, however measured, anticipated from the proposed investment must be evaluated and compared on some basis with the amount of funds the project will absorb. This is not a new problem and, consciously or unconsciously, such problems have been solved in one way or another ever since man first conceived the idea of investing money in business operations. In the past, the answer may have been the result of a simple process of intuition, or the result of one of the more traditional methods of investment appraisal.

Modern business is a complex organization, and personal vision or intuition has, in general, given place to more scientific methods of management by groups of people. This sharing in the decision-taking process requires some discipline in the methods that are used. This means that not only are more precise methods of reaching decisions required, but also that they should conform to a pattern that will enable them to be understood by the management team as a whole. This process applies equally to methods of comprehension and appraisal of capital investment. Prior to the introduction of DCF, the two methods that had been developed, and are still widely used, were the *accounting rate of return* and the *pay back period*. Before discussing the implications of DCF it will be useful to look at these two methods to see how effective they have been in ranking investments in order of profitability, and the deficiencies that have led to the search for a more effective method.

Accounting Rate of Return Method

This is a method that employs the normal accounting and budgeting techniques to measure the increase in profit expected to result from a new investment. This return is then compared with the amount of capital the project requires. The measurement of cost and income changes that will take place employs techniques familiar to people who are used to handling accounting data, and is, therefore, a method readily understood. No problems arise from the time phasing of the net return, the recording of this change being taken into the accounting period of the business in which profits are normally recorded.

Let us assume that the Board of Directors of X Ltd is considering the investment of £10 000 in a new automatic packing machine. An investigation of cost changes that would flow from the installation of the machine would be made. Let us assume that these cost changes would increase the net income of the business (after depreciation) by £1500 a year. The accounting rate of return for this project can then be expressed as the percentage of the cost of the machine that this addition to income represents. In

10

the case given, the percentage return would be $1500 \times 100/10\,000 = 15$ per cent.

So far, this is quite straightforward, but is it the proper measurement to use? The percentage return has been calculated on the original investment of £10 000. If, however, we assume that depreciation is written off in equal instalments over the life of the machine the amount invested will decrease each year as funds are released from the project through the effect of the depreciation charge. This decrease in the amount invested is shown in Fig. 1.2. At the end of the first year, the capital invested is reduced to £9000, if we assume a ten-year life for the machine. At the end of the second year, it will be reduced to £8000, and so on, reducing to zero at the end of the tenth year. If we further assume that the funds flow evenly over time, and not in annual steps as shown in Fig. 1.2, then the amount invested at any time would be given by the broken line shown in the figure.

It can be seen from this that the *average* amount invested over the whole life of the machine would be of the order of £5000, and on this basis the accounting rate of return would be given as $1500 \times 100/5000 = 30$ per cent.

Both the calculations made so far have been on a 'before tax' basis. They may both, also, be calculated on an 'after tax' basis. Overall, this would give (in the case of a company) an annual earnings rate of £1500 less 50 per cent corporation tax, or £750. The annual amounts of after tax earnings

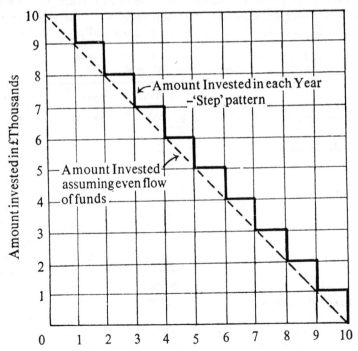

Figure 1.2. Amount invested in a fixed asset over its life

11

may differ from the even pattern of £750 a year, due to the substitution of capital allowances for depreciation in the tax computation, as will be discussed in chapter 3. The after tax earnings would, however, still average £750 a year and would give rates of return of 7·5 per cent on the original capital invested, and 15 per cent on the average capital invested.

Deficiencies of the Accounting Rate of Return

The difficulties of interpretation outlined in the previous two paragraphs could be overcome by adopting some common convention for calculating both the capital invested and the annual earnings, but there are even more serious objections to the use of this method.

If all projects to be considered had the same length of life and a level flow of profits over that life, this method might well provide a simple basis for comparison. But in real life this does not happen. Management will be faced with the problem of selecting from a number of projects showing varying patterns of earnings and varying lengths of life. Can this method cope with such disparities between the projects that it is trying to evaluate?

To find out whether it can, let us assume that the board is presented with three projects out of which it must select only one for approval. The amounts to be invested and the annual increases in profits likely to flow from the investments are shown in Table 1.2. The accounting rate of return shows each of these three projects as having the same rate of return. On this basis, management would be indifferent in choosing between these projects. But can it really be said that these three projects are equally profitable?

TABLE 1.2. *Comparison of Three Projects by the Accounting Rate of Return Method*

	Project A	Project B	Project C
Amount of investment	£10 000	£10 000	£10 000
Increase in profit (after depreciation)	£	£	£
Year 1	200	2300	1500
Year 2	1500	2000	1500
Year 3	1500	1500	1500
Year 4	2000	1500	1500
Year 5	2300	200	1500
Year 6	—	—	1500
Total profits	7500	7500	9000
Life of project	5 years	5 years	6 years
Average annual increase in profits	1500	1500	1500
Rate of return:			
On original investment	15%	15%	15%
On average sum invested	30%	30%	30%

If Project B is compared with Project A, it can be seen that the profits arising from B, on balance, come much earlier in the life of the project than those of Project A. The funds released by the earlier accrual of profits can be put to work to earn more profits through investment in other projects and, because of this earning power, are more valuable to the business than are profits arising in later years. In other words, there is a *time differential* in the earnings of these two projects that must be taken into account if a true comparison between the projects is to be made. The accounting rate of return, however, does not allow us to measure the effect of this time differential.

In Project C, another area of difficulty is encountered. It has a longer life than the others although the accounting rates of return are the same. How can we compare this additional year's earnings with the earnings patterns of the other two projects? So far, we have no method of assessment that will allow us to take this factor into account. What is needed is a a system that will take into account both the timing and the life differentials of a series of investment proposals and will incorporate the effect of these into the rate of return.

Pay Back Period

In order to avoid some of the pitfalls that we have seen to exist in the accounting rate of return method, and recognizing that the recoupment of the original capital invested in a project is an important element in its appraisal, a further method was evolved, known as the *pay back period*. The basic element of this method is a calculation of the time it takes to recoup the expenditure made on the project.

Various methods have been used to calculate the annual pay back, including before tax profits and after tax profits. But perhaps the most common basis used has involved the calculation of the *cash flow* arising from the project in each of the years of its life. This concept of cash flow will be more fully dealt with in chapter 4, but essentially it is a measure of the amount of cash that will be released from the project and become available for use in other areas of the business. This will be defined as the profits before depreciation and tax attributable to the project, adjusted for the capital allowances the business will receive as a consequence of the investment, and the net tax that will be payable on the profits so adjusted. The cash flows from each of these factors will also be related to the year in which it will occur rather than the period in which it is entered into the books of account.

When used in this way the pay back method requires the accumulation of the cash flows, year by year, until they equal the amount of the original investment. The length of time this process takes gives the pay back period for the project. As an illustration of the process, assume that the board of directors of AB Ltd are considering investing the sum of £10 000 in additional machining facilities for the company. The cash flows expected to arise from the project are detailed in the second column of Table 1.3.

At the end of the first year's life of the investment the company will have recouped £1000 of its original outlay on the project. By the end of the second year £2200, and so on, until the end of the fifth year when the whole of the £10 000 originally invested will have been recouped. In the example given, the project would be said to have a five-year pay back period.

TABLE 1.3. *Calculation of the Pay Back Period*

Amount invested in the project £10 000

Cash flows:

Year	Annual	Cumulative
	£	£
1	1000	1 000
2	1200	2 200
3	2000	4 200
4	3000	7 200
5	2800	10 000

Pay back period—five years.

It will be observed that this method makes no attempt to measure the return on the capital invested. All it provides is the length of time that it takes to recoup the amount expended on the project, the assumption being that projects with a short pay back period are better investment propositions than those with long pay back periods. The great disadvantage of this method, however, is that it takes no account at all of cash flows arising *after* the pay back period has been completed.

The effect of this can be considered by taking the case of a management selecting one of two investment proposals. Each proposal involves the investment of £10 000 and the annual cash flows from each are as detailed in Table 1.4. Project A has an anticipated life of only four years, and Project B is expected to have a life of ten years.

Project A has a pay back period of four years, which coincides with the termination of the project, there being no further cash flows. Project B has a pay back period of just over six years, but its cash flows continue beyond this period for another four years. On a strict comparison of the pay back periods, the decision of management would be to give approval to Project A, since this is the one with the shortest pay back period. This, however, is no criterion of the *profitability* of the project. Nothing in the method used enables a comparison to be made between the total return of £10 000 from Project A over its four-year life, and the total return of £16 100 from Project B over its ten-year life.

14

TABLE 1.4. *Comparison of Two Projects by the Pay Back Method*

Investment Cash flows: Year	Project A £10 000 Annual	Cumulative	Project B £10 000 Annual	Cumulative
	£	£	£	£
1	2 000	2 000	1 000	1 000
2	3 000	5 000	1 200	2 200
3	3 000	8 000	1 500	3 700
4	2 000	10 000	2 000	5 700
5	—	—	2 300	8 000
6	—	—	1 800	9 800
7	—	—	1 800	11 600
8	—	—	1 800	13 400
9	—	—	1 700	15 100
10	—	—	1 000	16 100
Pay back period	4 years		$6\frac{1}{9}$th years	

A close examination of the two projects, however, shows that Project A does nothing more than replace the funds originally invested. Therefore, the earnings rate on this project must be 'nil'. Project B, on the other hand, has a cumulative cash flow of £16 100, which more than replaces the funds originally invested and, therefore, must have a positive rate of return; but by using this method of appraisal, we have no means of knowing what that rate is.

Clearly, we have not progressed at all in our search for a method of arriving at a truly comparable rate of return, and the importance of the timing of receipts has once again been highlighted. The pay back method may have some uses, however, in situations where there may be a strict time limit to the investment before its otherwise useful life has been completed. If, for example, we are considering an investment in a project in an overseas country where the political stability can be foreseen for only a limited number of years, or when we are investing in plant involving processes or products that are likely to be replaced or revolutionized by technological change within a few years, then the pay back period will be a very relevant consideration in deciding whether or not to go ahead.

Any consideration of the pay back period should, however, never lose sight of the fact that bare recoupment of the amount invested would give a 'nil' earnings rate on the capital invested and, if it is used at all, there should be built into the calculations a rate of interest, or return, on the capital outstanding in each of the years involved.

Residual Value

The above discussions on the accounting rate of return and the pay back period have not taken into account another important factor in calculating profitability: that is, the cash flow that arises from the residual or scrap value of the project at the end of its life. In most cases there will be an inflow of funds from this source when the project is terminated and the remaining assets dispersed, and this inflow should be taken into account in any investment appraisal.

The amount involved may be insignificant, as when there is only the scrap value of worn-out plant to be taken into account. In other cases it may well be substantial, particularly if a large part of the original investment was in the form of stock and work in progress, and debtors. The whole of the value of such assets will be released from the project when it terminates, in addition to the scrap value of the plant. Any method of appraisal that ignores this factor can give, at best, only an imperfect indication of the rate of return earned.

Conclusions

What is needed by management to rationalize its investment decisions is a system that will enable it first to quantify the amount of capital that will be locked up in an investment. It must then be able to calculate the cash flows that can be expected in each year of the project's life, including any residual values. Having established both these factors it must then be possible to effect a comparison between the two in such a way that will take into account the timing of the cash flows, and to arrive at a ranking in order of profitability.

To sum up then, any method of appraisal of capital investments will have a vital role to play in maintaining or increasing the profitability of the business, both because of the long-term nature of such projects and the size of the funds that will be involved. The profitability of investments is just as important as the volume of investment, and within the individual firm the profitability factor will determine, to some extent, the volume of funds the firm will have available for investment in the future.

A high level of long-term profitability can be achieved only by a primary allocation of funds employed in the business, which should be determined at Board of Directors level, in order to maximize the possibility of achieving the objectives of the business. Within this overall allocation of funds there must then be a system of specific allocations to projects that will enable those projects offering the highest rates of return to be selected.

The more traditional methods of selection—the accounting rate of return and the pay back period—have serious disadvantages when considered in this context. On their own, they do not fully take into account all the factors involved in an investment decision, and in many cases may be completely misleading unless subject to further analysis. One factor of fundamental importance to investment decisions and one that has not been taken into account by either of the methods discussed, is the timing of profits and cash flows that result from an investment. It is this factor to which we must now turn our attention, since it is crucial to an understanding of the basis of discounted cash flow.

2 Present Value

The timing of cash flows has been seen to be the key to any satisfactory measurement of the return on investment. In this chapter it is proposed to examine the implications of this timing basis and of the time value of money.

Time Value of Money

In the private sector of the economy, funds are employed with the objective of earning a profit or increasing their value in some way. Within the individual business this will usually be accomplished by investing those funds in revenue-earning projects. Each of these projects will go through a cycle of events. First, funds are invested in the project and are not then available for other uses. This is followed by a period during which funds will be gradually released from the project through the earning of after-tax profits, and by the effect of depreciation. Finally, any residual value of the project will be released and the project terminated.

Any number of such projects, at different stages of the cycle, will be in being at any one time, the funds released from the projects that have reached a revenue-earning stage being applied to new projects that have been approved by management. The business will have at its disposal each year, quite apart from the injection of new capital resources, all the funds released in this way, and management will attempt to redeploy those resources in other profit-earning uses.

It is because of this earning capacity of the funds available to the business that their timing is of importance to management. The earlier they are made available, the sooner they will be making a further contribution to profits from their new employment. When any capital investment project is in process of discussion and evaluation, the time at which funds will be released will have a direct bearing upon its profitability, and this factor must be incorporated into the project evaluation.

Pattern of Cash Flows

The pattern of cash flows associated with any project can be represented in the form of a cash flow diagram, as shown in Fig. 2.1. In the base year

18

for the project (represented in the figure by Year 0) there is a movement out of the business of funds representing the amount of capital invested in the project. In the subsequent years (shown as Years 1–6), there is a cash flow back into the business measured by the after-tax earnings from the project, plus depreciation, and any residual value at the end of the life of the project.

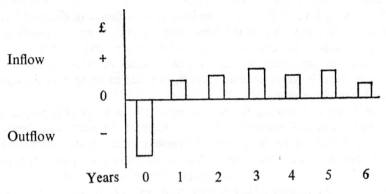

Figure 2.1. Cash flow diagram – simple project

The pattern of cash flows shown in Fig. 2.1 represents a fairly simple case. Other investment projects may be of a much more complex character. The construction of buildings and the installation of plant and machinery, in the case of a large project, may take several years to accomplish. Further, the initial plans for the project may include arrangements for increasing the capacity of the plant at various stages in its life. This is represented by the diagram, Fig. 2.2, in which the cash flows represented allow for a construction period of three years before the project is ready for operations, indicated in the figure by the years −2, −1, and 0. The project starts to earn profits in Year 1 and continues in subsequent years, with the exception of

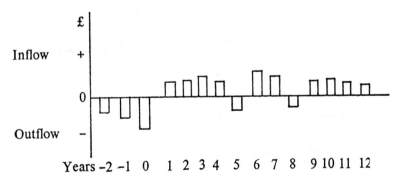

Figure 2.2. Cash flow diagram – complex project

19

years 5 and 8 when the installation of additional capacity results in a net cash outflow, the expenditure on the new plant exceeding the returns from the existing plant.

Whether the investment project is a complex or a simple one, the objective in using DCF is the same, namely, to relate the cash flows arising from the project to a common base year—the year represented in Figs. 2.1 and 2.2 by Year 0. Cash flows arising in years subsequent to Year 0 will need to be brought back to their value at the base year by means of discount factors that will reduce the value of the *future* receipts to their *present values* at the base year. Where the construction period for the project extends for more than one year, an interest or earnings factor must be *added* to the cost of the investment in years prior to Year 0, in order to bring it to the correct value for the base year.

This process of relating the cash flows of all the years of a project to a base year value is illustrated in Fig. 2.3. Each of the years' cash flows are *discounted* back to the base year, the present values being represented by the shaded areas. The cash flows for Year 1 and subsequent years are *reduced* by the discount factors, which represent the earning power of the cash flows in the intervening years. Expenditure prior to Year 0 is *increased* by the interest or earnings charge to bring it to base year values, so that the project bears the cost of the funds during the period they are locked up in the project and not earning a return.

The test of profitability for the project will then lie in the relationship between (1) the total of the positive cash flows that will be arising in the future at their base year values, (2) the total of the negative cash flows also brought in at base year values, and (3) the percentage rate that has been

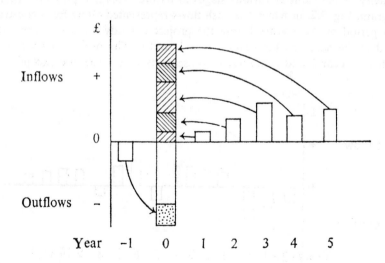

Figure 2.3. Process of relating cash flows to base year values

20

used to discount the cash flows in the calculation of their present values. The DCF technique is basically the appraisal of these three elements in such a way as will enable management to either (*a*) ascertain the rate of return that will be earned on the project, or (*b*) rank a series of projects in order of profitability.

Compound Interest

Money can be put to use in many ways. It can be deposited with a building society, bank, or other financial institution. It can be loaned to individuals or companies so that they can then use the money as part of the capital they are employing in their business. In all such cases, the person who loaned the money will expect some return for its use, the usual form of return being the payment of interest, or, in the case of shareholdings in companies, a dividend. The owner of the funds may, on the other hand, decide to use the funds in his own business where he would expect to obtain a return, in the form of an increase in the profits earned.

In all instances of funds being put to use, as distinct from hiding them under the mattress or holding them in a non-interest earning form, such as a current account, there is a common characteristic. The owner of the funds anticipates that they will increase in value over time through the accretion of interest or profit until such time as the funds are withdrawn for use in some other way, e.g., for investment in another use, or for consumption.

If £100 is deposited with a local authority, where it can earn interest at 7 per cent (ignoring for the time being the effects of taxation), at the end of one year the original £100 will have grown to £107, if the interest is calculated at yearly intervals. If this interest is not withdrawn but is left to accumulate, then at the end of the second year the original capital will have grown from £100 to £114·49 ($107 + 7 \times 107/100$). This process of accumulation will continue until such time as the funds are withdrawn from this particular use. In other words, the earnings on this investment are being allowed to accumulate in the form of compound interest. If it is required to be known to how much £100 (or any other sum) will grow over any period of time at any interest rate, the following formula can be used:

Let $i =$ interest rate per period, and
$n =$ number of periods.

Then,

$$\text{future value} = \text{present value} \times (1 + i)^n$$

Compound interest may be used in the solution of a number of business problems. Suppose that funds are available for investment in stocks of raw whisky which would be sold, after being held for five years, for the purpose of blending. It would be expected that the sale of the whisky at the end of the fifth year would realize more than the raw spirit cost, since over that period of time the capital locked up by the purchase would be expected to earn a return. If the funds could earn 8 per cent in other forms of investment, it would not pay to put one's money into this particular form of investment unless it could give a return of at least the 8 per cent it could earn elsewhere. If it is proposed to invest £1000 in this venture, then the realizable value of the whisky after five years would need to be in excess of £1470, which is the amount to which £1000 would grow in five years if earning 8 per cent compounded annually.

Similarly, where a business must make provision for the payment of a substantial lump sum of money at some time in the future, it will want to know what sum to put aside annually, which, when compound interest is added, will provide the sum required.

Present Value

Present value is calculated on the same basis as compound interest. Compound interest takes a present value and looks forward to see what sum that value will have grown to at some time in the future. Present value takes a sum receivable in the future and looks backwards to the present time to ascertain what the original sum would have had to be to grow to the future value.

If a business can earn 10 per cent on the funds it employs in the business, then, over a number of years, the original sum of £100 invested would grow in the following way:

Year 0	Year 1	Year 2	Year 3	Year 4	Year n
£100	£110	£121	£133·1	£146·41	$100(1+0·1)^n$

In such a case, a person or a business that could earn 10 per cent on their money would be indifferent whether it has £100 now, receives £110 in one year's time, or £121 in two years' time, and so on, because at an interest rate of 10 per cent these receipts are all of equal value to the owner when they are adjusted for the timing of the receipt. This criterion, of course, takes into account only the *time value* of money. It does not take into account inflationary trends in money values, or other uncertainties, which will be dealt with at a later stage. All we are doing at the present time is to examine preferences between the receipt of money at different times, on the basis of the earning power the money possesses.

The case where £100 will have grown to £110 at the end of one year is represented in Table 2.1 at (*a*), £100 invested on 31 December 1972 having grown to £110 by the end of the following year. But just as interest or earning power can be used to calculate future values, so a similar system can be used to take an amount receivable in the future and calculate its *present value*. This is the method known as *discounting*.

To say that £100 receivable now will have become £110 in one year's time is the same as saying that £110 receivable in one year's time has a present value of £100. Instead of looking forward from the present time to a time in the future, as shown at (a) in Table 2.1, we are merely taking a future time and relating it back to the present, as shown at (b). In order to arrive at a common basis for such calculations a further step can be made. If £110, receivable in one year's time, has a present value of £100, then £1 receivable in one year's time is worth £100/110, or £0·909 now, since if £0·909 is invested now and earns 10 per cent, it will have grown to £1 by the end of one year.

This relationship between present and future values can now be explored further. Table 2.1 sets out the basic relationships between the two for a period of one year. Now consider a range of years. Continuing with a 10 per cent rate of interest, we have already seen the value to which £100

TABLE 2.1. *Relationship between Present and Future Values*

		1972		1973
		£		£
(a)	100	$\longrightarrow$	110
(b)	100	$\longleftarrow$	110
(c)	$\dfrac{100}{110}$	$\longleftarrow$	1
(d)	0·909	$\longleftarrow$	1

TABLE 2.2. *Present Value of £1 receivable at Varying Times in the Future*

Year	Present value of £1 at 10% after the number of years	Year 0	Year 1	Year 2	Year 3	Year 4
		(£100)	(£110)	(£121)	(£133·1)	(£146·41)
0	£1 $\longleftarrow$ $\dfrac{100}{100}$ $\leftarrow$ £1					
1	£0·909 $\longleftarrow$ $\dfrac{100}{110}$ $\longleftarrow$ £1					
2	£0·826 $\longleftarrow$ $\dfrac{100}{121}$ $\longleftarrow$ £1					
3	£0·751 $\longleftarrow$ $\dfrac{100}{133\cdot1}$ $\longleftarrow$ £1					
4	£0·683 $\longleftarrow$ $\dfrac{100}{146\cdot41}$ $\longleftarrow$ £1					

23

would grow over a series of years. Using the same process as was used in Table 2.1 we can now relate these sums to present values and arrive at a common basis for all calculations—the present value of £1. This is shown in Table 2.2.

For a mathematical calculation of the present value of a future sum the following formula may be used:

$$\text{Present value} = \frac{\text{future sum}}{(1+i)^n}$$

where i = interest rate per period, and
n = number of periods.

USE OF DISCOUNT TABLES

The rather tedious method of discounting future values by means of the formula given in the previous paragraph can be avoided by using discount tables such as that shown in Appendix A. This shows the present value of £1 receivable at varying intervals of time and for a wide range of interest rates. To use this table, first find the column of factors that represents the rate of interest or return required. Then, follow this column down to find the line that corresponds with the number of years that must elapse before the money is to be received. The factor at the point where the column and line intersect is the factor by which the future sum must be multiplied to find its present value.

Take an example where a sum of £250 will be received after a period of eight years, and the rate of return is 6 per cent. First, locate the 6 per cent return column, then follow it down until the line for eight years is reached. The factor at this point is 0·627. Therefore, the present value of £250 receivable in eight years' time is £250 × 0·627 or £156·75.

When the same sum is receivable in each of a series of years, then, instead of discounting each year's receipt individually, the table given in Appendix B can be used. This table shows the present value of £1 receivable *annually*, again for a range of years and for a range of interest rates. To find the present value of £54 receivable in each of the next ten years, using an earnings rate of 8 per cent, first find the column for 8 per cent, then follow it down until the line for the tenth year is reached, which shows a factor of 6·710. To find the present value of £54 receivable annually for ten years, multiply that sum by the factor, e.g., £54 × 6·710 = £362·34.

Rate of Return

One method of using DCF is known as the *internal rate of return method*, sometimes called the *time-adjusted return* or *project rate of return*. This method involves calculating the rate of return it is estimated will be earned on the amount of capital invested in the project over its life. The calculation can be carried out by comparing the amount invested in the project with the cash flows that will be released from the project over its life. The pattern of cash flows to be compared will be similar to those shown in Figs. 2.1 and 2.2. That is to say, there will be an investment of funds initially, followed by a sequence of cash flows over the life of the project.

The aim of the rate of return method is to find a percentage rate of discount that will reduce the present values of the sequence of inwards cash flows to the same value as the cash invested in the project. The higher the percentage rate of discounting that is used the lower will be the present value of the cash flows. The lower the percentage used, the higher will be the sum of the present values. By a process of trial and error a percentage rate can be ascertained that will equate the present value of the cash flows from the project with the value of the cash investment. When this rate is found, it will be the rate of return earned on the funds invested in the project.

METHOD OF CALCULATING THE RATE OF RETURN

As an example of this process, take a case where the investment of £200 now will result in cash flows of £115 arising in each of the next two years, and we need to know the rate of return that will be earned on the funds invested.

In each of the two year's life of the project, there are inward cash flows (the time scale for the whole project will be: Year 0 invest £200, Year 1 receive £115, Year 2 receive £115, end of project). Each of the two year's cash flows must now be brought down to their present values as at the base year. By a method of trial and error, it will be found that using a discount rate of 10 per cent will bring their present values to a sum that equals the amount of the original investment.

A useful layout for this type of problem is given in Table 2.3, and will be used throughout this book. It is not the only way of setting out DCF problems—other layouts are equally useful—but a standardized layout will avoid the possibility of confusing the reader, and for that reason has been adopted here.

TABLE 2.3. *Calculating the Rate of Return*

Year	Cash flow	Present value factors for 10%	Present value
	£		£
1	115	0·909	105
2	115	0·826	95
			£200
Original sum invested			£200

The sum of the present values of the cash flows for the two years equals the amount invested, therefore the rate of return is 10 per cent

25

The first two columns of Table 2.3 show the identifying year and the cash flow for that year. The third column gives the discount factors for the 10 per cent rate for one and two years, ascertained from the present value table in Appendix A. These factors are then multiplied by the cash flows for their respective years to arrive at the present value of that year's cash flow. The two present values are then added, and the the total present value compared with the amount originally invested. As these two figures are the same, the rate of return earned on the investment must be the percentage rate used for discounting the cash flows, i.e., 10 per cent.

MEANING OF THE RATE OF RETURN

What exactly is meant when it is said that the rate of return on a project is X per cent? The rate of return can be defined as *the percentage earned on the amount of capital invested in each year of the life of the project after allowing for the repayment of the sum originally invested*. An understanding of what this definition implies is essential if DCF is to be fully understood in its application to business problems. At this stage, it is appropriate to examine in greater detail the example that has just been used.

One means of examining the truth of the definition given is to take an original investment of £200 and divide it into two factors: £105 invested for one year, and £95 invested for two years. The £105 invested would have grown to £115 by the end of one year and would then be withdrawn. This corresponds with the first year's cash flow of £115. The £95 invested would have grown to £105 by the end of one year and £115 by the end of the second year. This is now withdrawn, and corresponds with the second year's cash flow of £115. Taking the two components together, it can be seen that the original investment of £200 has earned 10 per cent on the sums invested in each year, in addition to providing the cash to replace the sum originally invested.

Another way of analysing the definition, and one that is perhaps much more familiar, is to treat it as a loan that is followed by a series of repayments comprising both interest and capital repayments, as happens with a building society mortgage. If it is assumed that a loan of £200 is made at 10 per cent interest to be repaid in two equal instalments of £115 at the end of one and two years respectively, the transaction would be represented as shown in Table 2.4. (As before, the figures have been rounded off to the nearest whole numbers.)

This analysis of the payments shows that the two years' cash flows (in this case the two loan repayments) provide for the repayment of the £200 originally lent *and* the provision of 10 per cent interest on the amount of the principal outstanding in each of the years.

An alternative definition is that if the cost of the 'pool' of funds (or capital employed) to the business is, say, 10 per cent, then a project that

TABLE 2.4. *Analysis of Cash Flows*

			£
Amount loaned			200
Year 1	Amount repaid	115	
	of which £20 (10% on £200) represents interest	20	
	leaving to be paid off the capital sum	95	
			95
	Amount still owing carried forward to Year 2		105
Year 2	Amount repaid	115	
	of which £10 (10% on £105) represents interest	10	
	leaving to be paid off the capital sum	105	
			105
	Amount owing after the second year		nil

has a rate of return of 10 per cent just covers the cost of the funds locked up in that project during its life.

Having established the general method of calculating the rate of return it will now be useful to look at a more complex problem in some detail, to see how the method works in practice.

Example 2.1
The Board of Directors of Wendover Ltd is discussing the possibility of purchasing a new lathe for £2000. The accountant has estimated that as a result of the savings that would ensue from the purchase of the lathe the cash flows of the company would be increased as follows:

Year	Cash flow
	£
1	500
2	500
3	600
4	600
5	440
Total	2640

Before reaching a decision, the directors have asked that the rate of return that will be earned on the project should be calculated.

PRE-ESTIMATE OF RATE OF RETURN
The process of establishing the rate of discount that will reduce the values of the cash flows so that their total value will equal the cost of the investment can only be a process of trial and error. Where the pattern of cash flows

is not too uneven, it is possible to arrive at some idea of the probable range of rates within which the solution will lie. This will reduce the area of 'search' for a rate. The method of calculating this approximation to the rate where it is appropriate is as follows. First, total the cash flows and ascertain by how much they exceed the amount of the original investment. Divide this excess by the number of years' life of the project. Finally, calculate what percentage the resulting figure represents of *half* the amount of the original investment.

Taking the figures given in the preceding example, the estimate can be prepared as follows:

1. Excess of cash flows over original investment—£2640 − £2000 = £640
2. 1, divided by the number of years' life—640/5 = £128
3. 2, as a percentage of *half* the original investment

$$128 \times 100/1000 = 12 \cdot 8\%$$

Taking 12 per cent as the first approximation of the rate of return, we can now proceed to evaluate the details given in Example 2.1. The annual cash flows expected are inserted in the calculation in the appropriate years as shown in Table 2.5. The discount factors for the 12 per cent rate are extracted from the present value table in Appendix A, for years 1 to 5. The cash flows are then multiplied by the present value factors to arrive at the present value of each year's cash flow, as shown in the last column.

TABLE 2.5, *Example 2.1. Calculation of Present Values using 12% Rate*

Year	Cash flow	Present value factors for 12%	Present value
	£		£
1	500	0·893	446
2	500	0·797	399
3	600	0·712	427
4	600	0·636	382
5	440	0·567	249
		Total	1903

The sum of these present values, using the 12 per cent rate, is £1903, which is less than the amount originally invested. The 12 per cent rate is therefore too high, and a lower rate of discount should be tried.

If 8 per cent is now selected as the rate to be used for the next attempt, then, proceeding through the same stages as above, the calculation would be as shown in Table 2.6. In this case it is found that the sum of the present values is greater than the amount of the original investment. The rate of 8 per cent is therefore not high enough. Rates of 8 and 12 per cent bracket the actual rate of return and we must look for the solution between these two figures.

As the two present values calculated are a similar amount either side of the original investment we can now take a rate that is half way between the two rates already used. Proceeding as before, we now calculate the present values for the 10 per cent rate, as shown in Table 2.7. In this

TABLE 2.6, *Example 2.1. Calculation of Present Values using 8% Rate*

Year	Cash flow	Present value factors for 8%	Present value
	£		£
1	500	0·926	463
2	500	0·857	428
3	600	0·794	476
4	600	0·735	441
5	440	0·681	300
		Total	2108

TABLE 2.7, *Example 2.1. Calculation of Present Values using 10% Rate*

Year	Cash flow	Present value factors for 10%	Present value
	£		£
1	500	0·909	454
2	500	0·826	413
3	600	0·751	451
4	600	0·683	410
5	440	0·621	273
		Total	2001

TABLE 2.8, *Example 2.1. Division of Cash Flows between Interest and Repayment of Principal*

Year	Amount invested at beginning of year	Cash flow	10% interest on amount invested at beginning of year	Balance of cash to reduce amount invested	Amount invested at end of year
	£	£	£	£	£
1	2000	500	200	300	1700
2	1700	500	170	330	1370
3	1370	600	137	463	907
4	907	600	91	509	398
5	398	440	40	400	(2)

case, it is found that the sum of the present values is almost exactly the same as the amount originally invested, therefore the rate of return that would be earned on this project is 10 per cent.

Referring back to the definition of the rate of return, the above calculation means that the investment of £2000 on a new lathe would generate additional cash flows that would provide for a 10 per cent return of the funds invested in each year, and repay the original £2000 invested. A division of the cash flows between interest and principal along the lines used in Table 2.4, is given in Table 2.8. The small differences are due to rounding off the discount factors.

USE OF RATE OF RETURN METHOD

The rate of return method is used to calculate the actual earning power of funds invested in a project. When the relative merits of a series of investment projects are under consideration, calculating the rate of return for each of the projects will enable management to *rank* them in order of profitability, and enable the following two criteria to be applied to the projects:

1. Which are the most profitable?
2. Do the projects meet the minimum rate of return laid down by management?

In any given situation management now has at its disposal a means of allocating the funds of the business to projects in the optimum way.

Present Value Method

The rate of return method, while providing direct comparison of profitability between projects, and with the cost of capital, does require the actual rate of return to be calculated. This, by the use of trial and error methods, tends to be time-consuming, particularly if the project is a complex one. An alternative to the rate of return method is the *present value method*. This involves taking one of the two criteria for project selection, namely, that of meeting the minimum acceptable rate of return, and, using that rate, calculating the present value of the future cash flows.

If the sum of the present values calculated in this way is less than the amount of the original investment the project does not meet the minimum rate of return, and would be rejected. If the present values exceed the original investment, the project earns more than the minimum rate and would be an acceptable project. Having thus subjected the project to evaluation against the minimum rate of return criterion, an additional step must then be taken to rank projects in order of profitability. This is done by calculating a *profitability index.*

30

The minimum rate of return used in the present value method we will call the *criterion rate of return*. This rate will be established by management after a careful appraisal of the cost of capital to the business and the general level of profitability that management wishes to achieve. The cost of capital will be discussed in detail in chapter 9; it is, essentially, the cost to the business of the long-term funds the business employs. Such costs will be represented by interest on loans and debentures, dividends on preference shares, and the return on equity holders' funds the business would have to offer if it were to go to the market to raise new equity funds. For most of the cases that will be discussed, it will be the *average* cost of capital that will be considered, although there may be certain instances where it may be appropriate to consider the *marginal* cost of capital.

The cost of capital will, in general, give only the lower limit of the criterion rate of return. Management will not invest funds in projects giving a lower return that the cost of capital unless there are special considerations involved. Moreover, it is likely to set a higher criterion rate than the bare cost of capital, for two reasons. In most projects there is an element of uncertainty, greater in some than others, and management will want to provide a margin to cover this. In addition, funds may be invested in projects in which there can be no measurable return, such as canteens and recreational facilities. The general provision of funds must cover such investments.

Preferably, the criterion rate should be determined as a part of the long-range planning. In this way it is directly linked to the profitability requirements of that plan.

Another yardstick that may be used is the rate currently being earned on the capital employed in the business. If this rate is a satisfactory one, the management may decide to base its assessment of what the criterion rate ought to be on this factor, making whatever adjustments they think are appropriate for uncertainty and planned improvements in profitability.

USE OF PRESENT VALUE METHOD

Whatever the basis management has used for setting the criterion rate of return, the first step in evaluating a project by the present value method is to discount the cash flows arising in each year by that rate, in order to find the present value of the cash flows on that basis.

Example 2.2

The Chairman of Oakley's Ltd has been presented with a proposal to build an extension to the factory and equip it with new woodworking plant at a cost of £50 000. The building would be a temporary one and would be demolished after eight years.

After considering the proposal and the current rate of return on capital employed, the chairman called in his accountant and said to him, 'Before approving this investment I want to know what rate of return is being earned on the present capital employed in the business, and to be satisfied that the forecasts for this proposed investment show that it will earn a return at least 1 per cent higher than this figure.' After analysing the company's accounts, the accountant established that the company was currently earning 5 per cent, after tax, on its capital employed. The criterion rate of return for this project would therefore be 6 per cent.

The cash flows anticipated from the project are as follows:

	£		£
Year 1	7000	Year 5	9000
Year 2	8000	Year 6	9000
Year 3	8000	Year 7	8000
Year 4	9000	Year 8	8000

Using the present value method to evaluate the project set out in the example, the first step would be to detail the cash flows by the years in which they are to be received, and alongside each to insert the present value factors for 6 per cent. The present value of each year's cash flow is then calculated by multiplying the two, and finally the sum of the present values is found. These are detailed in Table 2.9, from which it can be seen that the total present

TABLE 2.9. *Example 2.2, Present Value of Cash Flows Using a Criterion Rate of Return*

Year	Cash flow	Present value factor for 6%	Present value
	£		£
1	7 000	0·943	6 601
2	8 000	0·890	7 120
3	8 000	0·840	6 720
4	9 000	0·792	7 128
5	9 000	0·747	6 723
6	9 000	0·705	6 345
7	8 000	0·665	5 320
8	8 000	0·627	5 016
Total	66 000		50 973

value of the cash flows amounts to £50 973. This sum is greater than the amount of the original investment (£50 000) and, therefore, it earns a rate of return higher than the criterion rate of 6 per cent used for the discount factors, and would be an acceptable project. If the sum of the present values, using the criterion rate, had been less than the amount of the investment the project would be rejected as not meeting the minimum rate of return.

So far, in using the present value method we have provided the answer to only one of the investment criteria, namely, whether the project meets the minimum return requirement. In no way has the use of this method provided a means of ranking the projects in order of profitability. The rate of return method provided the answer to this criterion by calculating the actual rate of return. Here we have no rate of return for the project and must devise another means of ranking projects in order of profitability. This we can do by means of the *profitability index*.

The profitability index is based on a comparison of the total present value of the cash flows with the amount of the original investment, and it is a measure of the percentage increase in the capital sum that the present values represent. The formula for the calculation is as follows:

$$\frac{\text{Present value of cash flows}}{\text{Original amount invested}} = \text{profitability index.}$$

Taking the figures used in Table 2.9, the profitability index of the project outlined in Example 2.2 would be:

$$\frac{\text{£50 973}}{\text{£50 000}} = 1\cdot0195 \text{ profitability index.}$$

From the formula, it can be seen that the higher the profitability index the higher is the return earned on the project. The lower the profitability index the less profitable the project, and when the index falls below unity the project fails to meet the criterion rate of return.

Summary

In this chapter, we have discussed the way in which the future cash flows for a project can be reduced to a series of present values, so taking into account the timing of the cash flows. The present values are arrived at by a process of discounting, and the discount tables have a direct relationship with compound interest. Money has an earning power over time, and it is this factor that is used in the DCF technique to evaluate an investment project.

The technique can be used in one of two ways:

1. To arrive at a rate of return for a project.
2. To arrive at the present value of the cash flows using a criterion rate of return, and then rank by means of the profitability index.

Both these methods are designed to enable management to evaluate a series of projects on the basis of selection of the most profitable and setting a minimum rate of return.

So far, the examples that have been used have been based upon given cash flows. In practice, one of the most difficult parts of DCF is in calculating the cash flows themselves, and we must now examine the factors that influence their determination. One of the basic factors influencing the final value of the cash flow is taxation, and, because of its importance, this must be dealt with in the next chapter.

3 The Implications of Taxation

At first sight, the introduction of such a specialized topic as taxation into a book that deals with a capital investment appraisal technique, may seem to be unnecessary. In almost every country today, however, the business-man is faced with a comprehensive system of taxation that impinges on the decisions he takes in his business. Decisions that in other respects might be the right ones, may turn out to be unsound when the effects of taxation are considered. It is questionable whether a business should be obliged to mould around tax considerations the methods it uses to carry out its function, rather than perform them in a way that is in keeping with com-mercial requirements. It must, however, be agreed that the business is obliged to accept the environment in which it operates, and an important part of that environment is the tax structure.

In dealing with the appraisal of a capital investment project a number of tax effects must be recognized. It will be almost universally true that a substantial part of the earnings of the project will be subject to payments to the revenue authorities. The proportion taken in taxation will often be high, and, because of the size of the payment, its timing is important. In the United Kingdom, for example, there may be a delay of over a year in the payment of tax on earnings. Other countries may have a system of current collection of tax, as in the USA. Whatever the method, any time differential between the earning of profits and the payment of tax on them must be taken into account in the project appraisal.

Apart from the taxation of profits, many countries provide a system of incentives for encouraging capital investment and for writing off the cost of capital assets against profits. In the United Kingdom, we have had a number of systems of investment allowances, cash grants and accelerated capital allowances. These incentives can have a dramatic effect on the profitability of a project.

In addition to those factors already mentioned, there is the possibility of attracting capital gains tax on the sale of assets connected with a project, and other less obvious taxation problems, such as the value added tax. Many countries, too, offer cash and tax incentives to attract new business into their territory. Such factors may be highly relevant in the choice of geographical location. Although management may need to call in taxation specialists for the more detailed tax aspects of any decision, the manager himself should have a broad appreciation of the implications of taxation for any decision and, in particular, the capital investment decision.

In order to provide this general appreciation of tax effects as they affect investment appraisal, the following discussion of taxation will be taken under three broad headings:

1. Taxation on income.
2. The system of incentives and reliefs relating to capital investments.
3. The taxation of capital gains.

These topics will not be developed into a specialized discourse on taxation, but confined to general terms and touching upon those aspects that must be taken into account when using DCF. Taxation today is a highly complex subject, and what is said here may not apply in special situations where professional advice should be sought.

Taxation of Profits

PARTNERSHIPS AND INDIVIDUALS

In the United Kingdom, the taxation of trading profits for a partnership or an individual is governed by the Income and Corporation Taxes Act, 1970, as amended. The tax on such income will, therefore, be in the form of income tax including, where appropriate, a surcharge on large incomes. Until recently, the importance of undertakings operating under this form of organization would not have warranted their inclusion in a book on DCF. One of the effects of the 'close company' provisions of the Finance Act, 1965, was to encourage a number of businesses that previously would have operated in the form of a limited company, to trade as partnerships or individuals.

Basis of Assessment and Payment of Tax—Continuing Businesses
Where a partnership has been trading for some years, the basis of assessment for the tax payable for any tax year is the taxable profits of the business for the accounting period that *ended* in the *previous* tax year. Income tax is the only tax payable other than capital gains tax, and the amount on which it is levied will be reduced by personal reliefs.

Assume that Mr *A* owns a business that has been conducted profitably for several years. For his accounting year, which ended on 31 December 1972, the accounting profits as adjusted for tax purposes amounted to £2000. The business is Mr. *A*'s sole source of income. For the tax year 1973/74, the assessment will be based on the £2000 profit for the year to 31 December 1972. The actual amount of tax payable will be at the basic rate of tax, subject to the personal allowances and reliefs available. The tax will be payable in two instalments on 1 January 1974 and 1 July 1974.

36

Most businesses not trading as corporations will therefore experience a delay between the time they earn profits and the time they have to pay the tax related to those profits. According to the year-end date of the business, the payment will fall due either in the following year or the year afterwards. This delay is significant and will have to be taken into account in the DCF calculation.

Basis of Assessment and Payment—First and Closing Years
For the tax year in which the business is started, the assessment to tax is based on the proportion of the taxable profits of the business for its first year, which relate to that tax year.

Example 3.1
Mr *A* starts trading on 1 January 1973, and his first accounting period ends on 31 December 1973. The taxable profits for that period amount to £4000.

For the tax year 1972/73 the assessment will be $\frac{1}{4}$ (three months) of £4000, or £1000.

For the tax year following that in which the business was set up, the assessment will be based on the taxable profits of the business for its first year's trading. Taking the details given in Example 3.1, the assessment on Mr *A* for the tax year 1973/74 will be £4000 being the taxable profits for the first twelve months' trading.

In the subsequent tax year, the basis of assessment reverts to the normal continuing basis, as set out previously. In this tax year there is now an accounting period that ended in the previous tax year. Mr *A*'s assessment for the tax year 1974/75 will be £4000, being the taxable profits for the accounting period, which ended in the previous year.

The first year's profits will generally, therefore, determine the tax liability for the first three years of the life of the business; the main exception is where the accounting period exactly coincides with the tax year, when it will form the basis of only two years' assessments. Where the profits of the business on an actual basis are less than the assessed profits for the second tax year, the taxpayer has the option to have the second and third years' assessments amended to the actual profits of those years.

In the closing years of the business, the final year's assessment is based on the taxable profits of the fiscal year in which trading ceased; if the sum of the penultimate and ante-penultimate years' assessments is a lower amount than the actual profits of those years, the Inland Revenue may revise those assessments to the actual profits of those years.

Rate
The current (1973) basic rate of tax is 30 per cent.

For the purposes of corporation tax, the term 'corporation' includes not only limited companies and other incorporated bodies, but also a number of un-incorporated bodies. It excludes entirely partnerships and individuals, who will continue to be taxed in the way already dealt with.

Basis of Assessment

The basis of assessment to corporation tax is the accounting period of the company. If the company's accounting year runs from 1 January to 31 December 1973, the profits for that period form the basis for the assessment for the taxation period running from 1 January to 31 December 1973. The period 1 January to 31 March 1973 falls in the corporation tax year 1972 (the corporation tax year is dated by the year in which it starts). The period 1 April to 31 December 1973 falls into the tax year 1973.

Where the rate of tax changes between corporation tax years, then the profits for an accounting period (unless it coincides with the tax year) are apportioned between the two periods falling in each of the two tax years that it straddles, and each of these portions is taxed at the relevant rate for that period.

Assume that ABC Ltd has taxable profits for the year to 31 December 1974 of £12 000. The corporation tax rate for the tax year 1973 is 50 per cent, and for the year 1974 it is 45 per cent. The tax on the profits of the company for the year to 31 December 1974 will be ascertained as follows:

	Taxable profits £	Tax rate %	Tax payable £
Corporation tax year 1973 ($\frac{1}{4}$ of £12 000)	3 000	50	1500
Corporation tax year 1974 ($\frac{3}{4}$ of £12 000)	9 000	45	4050
	12 000		5550

Rate

The current (1973) rate of corporation tax is 50 per cent. There are special provisions for small companies which earn less than £15 000. In their case, the rate is reduced to 40 per cent.

Timing of Payments

When companies were taxed under the income tax acts, the tax payable in respect of any tax year would have been payable in one sum on 1 January in the year of assessment. The profits that formed the basis of assessment would have been those earned in the accounting period ended in the previous tax year, as is still the case for individuals. This would mean that, for a company whose accounting period ended on 30 June 1964, the payment of tax on the assessment related to those profits would be made on 1 January 1966—a delay of eighteen months after the end of the accounting period.

While corporation tax assessments are based upon a current year basis, the same interval between the end of the accounting period and the *payment* of tax continues for companies in existence on 5 April 1965. If, for example, a company's accounting period ended on 30 September, there would have been a fifteen month delay in the payment of the tax based on any year's profits under the income tax system. This fifteen month delay continues under the corporation tax system. If the assessment is not raised until after this date, then the tax is due one month after assessment.

While the above rules apply to companies in existence on 5 April 1965, for those incorporated after that date, there is a standard period of nine months after the end of the accounting period or one month after assessment if later.

In situations where the UK type of system operates the implication for DCF is that there will always be a division between the year in which profits are earned and the year in which tax payments related to those profits are made. In some countries, such as the USA and France, this time delay has been virtually eliminated. In assessing cash flows, the timing of tax payments must be related to the requirements of the tax system under which the company operates, and, if different, where it is resident.

Capital Allowances (Depreciation)

The amount of depreciation that can be charged against taxable profits is normally subject to regulation. In the UK, for example, the amounts that are allowed are laid down in the taxing statutes, and these rates apply irrespective of the amounts included in the company's accounts. In other countries, this may be regulated by laying down in the tax regulations those depreciation methods and rates that are acceptable to the revenue authorities.

In addition to the regulation of depreciation allowances a number of governments provide special incentives, either to invest generally in industrial plant, etc., or to invest in specific industries or geographical areas. These incentives might take the form of *cash grants* towards the cost, or provide for *accelerated capital allowances*, i.e., a large part of the depreciation allowance is taken in the first or early years of the life of the asset.

DEPRECIATION

As far as the UK is concerned, whether one is taxed as an individual or a company, the depreciation charged in the accounts is disallowed for tax purposes. To arrive at the taxable profits for the year, the amount charged for depreciation must be added to the net profit as shown below:

XYL Ltd

Items extracted from the Profit and Loss Account

	£
Gross Profit	15 000
Depreciation	2 000
Other expenses	3 000
Net Profit	10 000

The taxable profit for XYL Ltd will be:

	£
Net profit as per accounts	10 000
Add back depreciation	2 000
	12 000

Two points emerge from this treatment of depreciation. First, under the UK type of system, the basis of depreciation adopted for the accounts will not affect the overall tax charged on the company. Second, when computing the cash flows for DCF, depreciation should not be deducted from the increased profits. Thus, the increase in profits before depreciation, i.e., the cash flow, equals the taxable profits before deducting capital allowances.

The capital allowance provisions in the UK are set out in the Capital Allowances Act, 1968, (as amended by subsequent Finance Acts). The provision of cash grants to direct new investment into certain geographical areas is set out in the Industry Act, 1972. (Agriculture has its own set of regulations.)

UNITED KINGDOM CAPITAL ALLOWANCES

The system currently in force (1973) provides for two levels of allowance, a special allowance in the year in which the asset is acquired, and annual writing down allowances in subsequent years. The rates allowed are set out in Table 3.1.

First Year Allowance

For plant and machinery this is the only allowance given in the year in which the asset is purchased. Industrial buildings and structures receive a similar allowance called an *Initial Allowance*.

Writing Down Allowance

In years subsequent to that in which a first year allowance or initial allowance is given, the statutes provide for an annual amount to be allowed based upon a percentage of the reducing balance for plant and machinery; a

40

TABLE 3.1. *First Year and Annual*
Writing Down Allowances in the UK (1972)

Type of capital expenditure	First year or initial allowances	Annual writing down allowances
1. *Plant and Machinery* (incl. vehicles other than private cars)		25%
27/10/1970 to 18/7/71	60%	
19/7/1971 to 21/3/72	80%	
After 22/3/72	100%	
2. *Ships and Industrial Equipment in a Development Area or* N. Ireland	100%	25%
3. *Expenditure on Scientific Research*	100%	
4. *Industrial Buildings & Structures*		
(*a*) Development Area and N. Ireland	40%	4% straight line
(*b*) Elsewhere Up to 21/3/1972	15%	4% straight line
22/3/1972 and after	40%	4% straight line
5. *Private Cars*	Nil	25%
6. *Mining and working Mineral Deposits*		
(*a*) Development Area and N. Ireland	100%	
(*b*) Elsewhere	40%	Output/Output + Potential future output

Notes: There is no obligation to take the whole of the first year or initial allowances. One can opt for only part of the total.

Except where specified the annual writing down allowances are on a reducing balance basis.

percentage straight line for industrial buildings; and upon a formulae calculation for mining and mineral deposits, all at the rates set out in Table 3.1.

Each group of assets goes into a common pool, e.g., all plant and machinery purchased after 27 October 1970 can go into a single pool account. This account is debited with the cost of all new plant purchased; it is credited with receipts from disposals, the first year's allowance on the current year's purchases, and the writing down percentage upon the opening balance in the pool account for that year, less the amounts received from any disposals.

Assume that the balance shown by the pool account at the end of the previous year was £345 786. During the year £1439 was received from disposals of plant and £92 638 was spent on new plant. If the first year allowance applicable for that year is 80 per cent, the record of written down values and allowances for the pool would appear as follows:

	£	£
Opening balance		345 786
Less disposals		1 439
		344 347
Additions during year	92 638	
Less: First year allowance at 80 per cent	74 110	
		18 528
		362 875
Less annual writing down allowance 25 per cent of £344 347		86 087
Balance being written down value carried forward to next year		276 788

The total capital allowances for the year will therefore be:

	£
First year allowance (80 per cent of new additions)	74 110
Annual writing down allowance	86 087
	160 197

BALANCING CHARGE

It will be noted from the above that when assets are sold or scrapped, any receipts from their disposal simply reduce the balance upon which the writing down allowances are computed. Only where this receipt exceeds the written down value of the pool is there any need for a special adjustment. In such a case, a balancing charge would be levied. This is a form of negative capital allowance amounting to the negative value on the pool account.

EFFECT OF GRANTS AND CAPITAL ALLOWANCES ON CASH FLOW

Cash flow computations must take into account the following factors related to the acquisition and ownership of fixed assets:

(a) Are there any direct financial subsidies available which will reduce the actual cost of the assets? The net cash investment must be reduced by the amount of any such receipts.

(b) Are there any methods of obtaining capital allowances early in the life of the asset such as the British first year allowance or other forms of accelerated capital allowances? If advantage can be taken of these, they will improve the cash flows in the early years where they are more valuable.

(c) What is the method of taking the year by year depreciation or writing down allowances? These reduce the taxable profits in the year in which they are taken and will therefore reduce the cash outlay for tax.

(d) When assets are disposed of, will there be any tax effects? Under the present UK system, receipts reduce the value of the asset 'pool' and therefore the stream of future capital allowances by the amount of the receipt. Where the pool value becomes negative, there is an immediate pull back of the amount of the deficit in the form of a balancing charge.

(e) What is the timing of the cash flow effects enumerated above? This will depend upon the tax payment timing already mentioned. Again, referring to the UK system, if tax is payable one year after the end of an accounting period, then the tax saving from capital allowances given for any year will not become effective until one year later, when that year's tax payment is made. Where tax is paid on a current basis with no delay, then capital allowances become effective in the year in which the expenditure on the assets takes place. Direct grants and subsidies are usually paid by governments and other agencies some time after the outlay took place.

UK FIXED ASSETS OWNED PRIOR TO 27 OCTOBER 1970

Assets owned before 27 October 1970 continue to be treated for tax purposes under the old rules and are not aggregated in the 'pool'. When they are disposed of, and the disposal forms an offset to the net cash investment, the tax implications must be taken into account.

The system provided that where an asset that has attracted capital allowances is sold then, if the sale value exceeds the written down value for tax purposes, the difference is taken back in the form of a balancing charge. If it falls short of the written down value, then the difference is given as an additional capital allowance called a balancing allowance. There was no pool concept and a separate record of the capital allowances for each item of plant had to be maintained.

Example 3.2

PR Ltd is installing new electric furnaces. The existing furnaces were installed some years ago and were given capital allowances under the old (pre-1970) system. Their written down value for tax purposes is £12 450, and it is expected that the scrap value will be £2000.

An additional capital allowance (balance allowance) will be given in the year of disposal computed as follows:

43

	£
Written down value at date of disposal	12 450
Receipt on disposal	2 000
Balancing allowance	10 450

If the old furnaces could have been sold for £15 000, a balancing charge would be made which would draw back the overprovision of capital allowances in earlier years. The computation would be as follows:

	£
Written down value	12 450
Receipt on sale	15 000
Balancing charge	2 550

CARRYFORWARD OF UNUSED CAPITAL ALLOWANCES

Where the business makes a loss or a level of profit insufficient to absorb the benefit of all the capital allowances available for that year, it is usually possible to carry forward any unused value to offset against future years' profits. It may also be possible to carry them backwards in time and offset them against profits that have already been taxed and so secure a tax repayment. For example, in the right conditions, first year allowances in the UK can be carried back three years.

As far as the cash flows are concerned, where the business is making losses or very low taxable profits, the cash flow effect of capital allowances must be postponed until profits are available to offset the capital allowances, unless it is possible to secure the repayment of tax already paid.

Capital Gains Tax

Where a business that is not liable to corporation tax realizes an asset for a sum greater than the cost to the business of that asset, there will be a liability to pay capital gains tax. Small disposals that realize less than £1000 on sale are excluded from these provisions. Where the project being appraised includes the sale of assets, whether replaced assets or those remaining at the end of the life of the project, this liability to capital gains tax must be given consideration. Taxable gains of companies are included in the corporation tax computation.

RATE OF TAX

The rate of tax payable by a corporation is the current rate of corporation tax, on three-fifths of the gain (some investment companies excepted).

For individuals and partnerships, the rate of tax is 30 per cent of the capital gain, or, if a lower rate, half the capital gain taxed at the individual's marginal rate for income.

ROLL-OVER PROVISIONS

There are special provisions in the Finance Act, 1965, relating to assets used in a trade. These are known as the *roll-over* provisions, the practical effect of which is that a business that is continuing (i.e., not being closed down) can carry forward the liability for capital gains tax for an indefinite period.

When the business is purchasing new assets, instead of paying the tax on capital gains realized in any one year, it can offset the capital gain against the cost of the new assets. This means that for purposes of capital gains tax, the cost of the new assets is effectively reduced, so increasing the ultimate liability on their sale in due course.

The roll-over provisions can be applied only to sales and purchases of assets within the same class. As, however, land and buildings and plant and machinery are all in the same class, this restriction should not have much practical effect, so far as capital investment projects are concerned.

The roll-over provisions may be carried on over an indefinite series of transactions, and the payment of capital gains tax deferred well into the future. Although its possible effects should not be forgotten when using DCF, this long postponement of the tax payment may make the liability irrelevant to the DCF solution.

Taxes and Subsidies in Respect of Employees

Within an individual country, there may be discriminatory taxes or subsidies in respect of employees. A recent example was the Selective Employment Tax in the UK, which discriminated between different industries. More usually there are selective subsidies to encourage employment in specified areas. These may be on a per capita basis or be given as grants towards training staff. The cash flow effects of such differentials will be relevant where the business is comparing the profitability of projects operating in different regions.

Where management is considering the country in which to set up a new plant such differentials may figure quite largely in the calculation.

Value Added Tax
(Taxe sur la valeur ajoutée)

This tax operates in similar ways throughout the community of nine including the United Kingdom. As far as the acquisition of fixed assets is concerned VAT will not effect the long-term cash flows of businesses that are not exempted from VAT. Although VAT will be added to the cost of a capital asset when it is purchased, this amount of VAT, together with the VAT on all other inputs will be set-off against the VAT the business has added to its own sales and will be recouped in this way. If the tax on inputs exceeds the tax on outputs, then the difference will be refunded by Customs and Excise.

Example 3.3

TVE Ltd buys £120 000 of new plant during 1974. The invoices for the plant have £12 000 VAT added. Other purchases during the year amount to £1·5 million on which £150 000 VAT has been paid. Sales for the year are £3 million to which the business will have added £300 000 for VAT.

The payments to the revenue authorities will be made up as follows:

	£	£
Tax on outputs (sales)		300 000
Tax on inputs:		
Fixed assets	12 000	
Other	150 000	
		162 000
Payments to Customs and Excise		138 000

It can be seen from the above that the tax collected from customers has been sufficient to refund the tax the company has paid leaving only a balance to be paid to the revenue. The only effect that VAT might have is to marginally affect the working capital requirements. Where the business is exempted from the VAT system, the VAT charged will add to the cost of the asset.

Conclusions

When appraising the merits of any capital project, the effects of taxation and other government intervention cannot be ignored. In spite of the specialization even among tax experts themselves, managers should have a broad appreciation of the possible tax consequences of any decision that they make. The more sophisticated analysis can be left to the professional, but the manager is working in the dark if he is not aware of possible tax consequences. This broad appreciation will enable him to call for proper advice at the right stage in the appraisal, before any final decision is made, rather than leave the taxation aspects to be sorted out later.

A variety of tax systems and capital incentives will be used in examples in the remainder of this book.

4 Determination of the Cash Flows

The Cash Flow

Those who are accustomed to reading reports on companies in the financial press will be familiar with the term *cash flow*. As applied to the reports on the financial affairs of companies this term covers the cash arising from the operations of the company for its financial year. This is of interest to investors and others as a measure of the funds that become available to management for further employment in the company and is the internally generated contribution to the pool of funds. This concept of cash flow is very similar to that used in the DCF technique.

In company reporting, the annual cash flow is taken as the after tax profits of the company *plus* the depreciation charge included in the accounts for the year after providing for the cost of the dividends payable. In this context, cash flow is a measure of the additional funds provided for the business by the retention of profits, plus those funds released from existing uses by the operation of depreciation charges. For a note on the relationship between depreciation and cash flow see Appendix C.

As used in DCF, cash flow will be defined as the after-tax profits of the project, plus the depreciation charge. DCF will, however, take into account differences in the *timing* of the components that make up the cash flow, whereas company accounts include them in the relevant accounting period. When setting out the calculation of the cash flow for the DCF, appraisal the major income and tax components must be shown separately and allocated to the years when the cash flow actually occurs.

This concept of cash flow is of vital importance to capital investment appraisal since the real cost to a business of any new investment project is the actual *net amount of cash* that flows out of the business as a result of the investment decision, and the return to the business on that project will be the actual amount of cash made available to the rest of the business from that project during its life.

Distinction between Cash Flow and Accounting Entries

The cash outlay on a new project may, in a number of cases, be the same as the book cost as shown in the accounts, and may also occur in the same accounting period. A new investment that consists solely of a simple addition to plant and machinery, as distinct from the replacement of an existing item of plant, will have cash flows and book entries that are equal in value since there are no other factors to consider. The cash outlay for the new purchase is a measure of its cost and as such would be recorded in the books of the business.

In many cases, however, this will not be true. When a project that involves the replacement of existing plant is being considered, the issue is not so clear cut. The cash out-flow for the new plant being purchased will be the same as the book value of that plant, as before, but the net cash receipts (if any) arising from the sale of the items that are to be replaced will now have to be taken into account. These receipts will consist not only of the receipts from the actual sale of the plant itself, but also of any cash flows resulting from the effects of taxation.

When considering the amount of the cash flows during the life of a project, the annual cash flows used for the DCF calculation will differ from the book values of after tax profits plus depreciation. This is not because different basic figures are used, but because the DCF cash flows will be allocated to the years in which the cash movement takes place, so that the time value of money is taken into account. In the accounts of the business, on the other hand, profits and taxes will be taken up in the accounting periods to which they relate. Overall for any project, the book values will equal the cash flows, as will be shown later in this chapter; the only difference will be in their timing.

Incremental Principle
The remarks so far in this chapter have highlighted an important principle upon which the determination of all DCF cash flows depends. That is, we are concerned with *incremental* cash flows, not absolute cash flows.

DCF, essentially, is dealing with problems of choice—shall we invest in this project or not? Shall we choose this alternative or that alternative? DCF appraises the alternatives open for each problem on the basis of the changes that will occur in the cash flows of the business as a consequence of choosing one alternative rather than another. If we make a choice to proceed with a particular investment, we must evaluate the net change in the cash position that will ensue from all the consequences of that decision, and not merely the purchase of the asset itself.

Consider the launching of a new product that is specifically designed to replace an existing ageing one, and that will use some of the business's existing facilities. The cash flows to be appraised will not be the sums spent on the new project, nor the cash flows from its earnings during its life. They will consist of the *extra* cash that will be invested in the project and the *additional* cash flows arising from the project over and above those from the existing product. The extra cash flows invested in the product as a result of the decision to proceed will consist of the outward payments for new plant, working capital, and so on, less those amounts that are released by discontinuing the old product. Both these changes are a result of the investment decision.

In the same way, the inwards cash flows generated by the new product will not be a measure of the cash flows resulting from the investment decision. The consequences of the investment decision are that the business gains the cash flows resulting from the new product and loses those resulting from the old product, and it is with the net difference that we are concerned.

Whatever the type of problem we are trying to solve by DCF, this incremental principle must always be borne in mind. One must examine *all* the consequences of the course of action that is proposed, and evaluate the cash flows resulting from each of the consequences so as to arrive at the net cash flows for that course of action.

Types of Cash Flow

The cash flows that must be quantified for the purpose of a DCF appraisal are as follows:

1. *Net Cash Investment.* This is a measure of the cost, in terms of cash resources to the business, of the new investment.
2. *Annual Cash Flows.* These represent the cash arising from the operations, etc., relating to the project, which provides for the recoupment of the original investment, plus the return (if any) that is earned by the project. For this purpose, the annual cash flows will be augmented by,
3. *Net Residual Value.* This is the net cash flow resulting from the disposal of the assets remaining in the project at the end of its life.

These three aspects of the cash flows will be treated separately in this chapter in order to provide a simpler framework for their calculation. Each of these types of cash flow requires quite different considerations to be taken into account in their evaluation, and it is useful to divide the framework for the overall solution into these three essential parts. Not only will it encourage clarity in thinking, but it will also enable the cash flows resulting from the operations of the project to be considered quite independently of considerations of net cash investment and residual value.

Net Cash Investment

The term *net cash investment* is used here to denote the net outflow of cash that will result from the investment decision. As such, it will be a measure of the volume of funds that the business is committing to that particular project, and against which its return will be measured. This concept of the 'cost' of an investment project is used rather than its book cost, because it is the return that will be earned on the net funds 'locked up' in a project that is relevant to our appraisal of different investment projects. For the business as a whole, the return on capital employed will be the sum of all the returns earned on the funds locked up in all their existing uses.

Acquisition of Assets

The principal component of the net cash investment will be the expenditure on the assets that are to be acquired for the project, including, where necessary, additions to working capital. Assets to be acquired include items of plant and machinery, buildings and land, together with the costs of installation, modification, and commissioning. When there is a 'running in' period, the cost of this process must also be taken into account, the principle here being that all cash expenditure involved in getting the project to a state where it is a functioning operating unit should be included.

The new project may involve the use of items of plant and machinery, buildings, and so on, that are already in the possession of the business and that, but for the decision to proceed with the project, would have been considered surplus to requirements, and sold. The realizable value of these assets must be included in the cost of the new project. Although there is, in fact, no actual cash outlay in respect of such items, the business is foregoing the receipt of cash from their sale, and, as a result of the new investment decision, will be that amount of cash worse off.

Similar considerations apply when the new project will use assets that otherwise would have been redeployed to other uses. Because these assets will not now be available, these other uses must now be satisfied by acquiring other machinery from outside the business, again involving the business in a cash outlay that is a consequence of the new investment decision.

Promotion Costs of New Products

The launching of a new product will involve the business in considerable outlays of cash for the purpose of market research and other promotional activities. These costs must be taken into account in the assessment of the net cash investment.

Working Capital

In addition to the employment of fixed assets on a project, there may also be a requirement for additional working capital. This is particularly so when the project is for the manufacture and marketing of a product additional to the business's existing product range. Estimates will have to be made of the additional stocks and work in progress that will be required, and of the additional funds needed to finance debtors.

The criterion as to whether stocks and debtors should be included in the net cash investment is whether or not the project involves any *additional* investments in these items over and above the levels already existing. The substitution of one form of working capital for another is not sufficient to warrant the inclusion of an amount for this item since the cash investment in the new project will be offset by the funds that are released from their existing uses.

Some projects may necessitate carrying stocks of spares. When this is so, the cash cost of such items must be included.

Treatment of Assets Replaced

One consequence of the investment decision may be that some assets the business already owns are no longer required, and will be disposed of. Typical of such a situation is when the principal objective of the new project is to replace plant and machinery with more modern equipment.

The disposal of the old equipment will result in a cash inflow to the business from the sale value which must then be adjusted for any tax consequences arising from the disposal. The net cash from the sale must then be used to reduce the cash expended on the new plant, to arrive at the value of the net cash investment.

Example 4.1

The Board of Directors of Seetops Ltd is considering the position of the company when the lease of its present factory expires. It is proposed to build a modern purpose-built factory in S.E. England to replace its existing premises. The cost of building and equipping the new factory will be £125 000, and on completion a quantity of old machinery will be sold and should realize £45 000. The new factory is expected to have an output 50 per cent greater than the old factory and will require an extra £25 000 investment in working capital to support this higher level of activity. Tax considerations are to be ignored at this stage.

On the details given in Example 4.1, the net cash investment for the new factory will be:

	£
Cost of new factory and plant	125 000
Less sale of old machinery	45 000
	80 000
Additional working capital	25 000
Net cash investment	105 000

The above treatment of replaced plant is appropriate if we are considering whether to replace existing plant or not. Different considerations will apply if the decision to replace has been taken, and we are considering which one of several alternative methods of replacement to use. In this situation, the cash value of the plant replaced is not a relevant factor since the cash value will be realized whichever of the alternatives is chosen. In this context, it cannot be considered as an incremental cash flow for any of the alternatives and would be ignored. (See chapter 6, 'Alternative Choice Problems'.)

TAX EFFECT ON VALUE OF PLANT REPLACED

When the net cash investment takes into account the cash resulting from the disposal of existing equipment, this cannot be considered without reference to the tax effect of such a disposal. As was seen in chapter 3, where plant, machinery or buildings are disposed of by the business, there will normally be a drawback of capital allowances already given or additional allowances above those already taken, and possibly a capital gains tax liability, to be taken into account. The net effect of these may be to increase or decrease the amount of cash realized from the sale. It is the net amount, after such an adjustment, that is relevant to the calculation of the net cash investment. Tax considerations will not, of course, affect the valuation of cash flows in respect of changes in working capital.

Example 4.2

Taking the same figures as were given in Example 4.1, the written-down value for tax purposes of the old machinery that is to be sold amounts to £25 000. (Assume that tax is paid at the small company rate of 40 per cent.) The old plant is all pre-1970.

The build up of the Net Cash Investment will now be affected by the balancing allowances/charges and will appear as follows:

Net Cash Investment	£	£
Cost of new factory and plant		125 000
Less Net proceeds of sale of old plant:		
Cash received	45 000	
Balancing charge:		
£20 000* at 40 per cent tax rate	8 000	
	——	37 000
		88 000
Additional working capital		25 000
		——
Total		113 000

* Sale value of £45 000, less written-down value of £25 000.

Development Grants

To encourage industry to move to certain geographical areas governments may make cash grants towards the cost of new capital equipment. The re-

52

ceipt of such grants may either be added to the cash flows for the year in which it is received, or treated as a reduction of the net cash investment. In the author's view, the latter method of treatment is to be preferred, as it allows all the factors that are connected with the determination of the net cash investment to be dealt with at the same time. This avoids the intrusion of extraneous factors when calculating the annual cash flows.

SELECTION OF THE BASE YEAR

When the period for the construction and installation of the new project is less than one year, it is usual practice to treat the year of installation as the base year, and in this book this year is denoted by Year 0. Year 1 will therefore be the year in which the operations of the new project begin.

When the construction and installation period is greater than one year, the usual practice is to designate the last year of the construction and installation period as the base year.

TIMING OF THE NET INVESTMENT CASH FLOWS

The time value of money is just as relevant to the valuation of the net cash investment as to other cash flows. This means that all the cash flows relating to the net cash investment must be allocated to the years in which the cash flow is expected to take place. The simple acquisition of a single item of plant will not normally involve cash flows outside the base year. More complex projects may have to take into account a number of other factors, the two principal being:

1. When the payments for the plant, etc., are made over a number of years due to the length of the construction period or through the operation of a retentions period by the contractor or supplier.
2. When the figures are significant, the tax adjustments consequent on the disposal of old plant and the acquisition of new plant, which will usually fall outside the base year, must be considered.

In 1 above, the cash payments that fall in years prior to the base year should have added to them compound interest at the DCF rate being used in order to bring them to their proper time value at the base year. When payments are made (or receipts due) after the construction period is complete, which consequently fall after the base year, these must be discounted to bring them back to the base year value.

Example 4.3

Taking the details used in Examples 4.1 and 4.2, it is found that the construction period for the project is two years, and it is expected that £60 000 of the cost will be paid in the first year and £65 000 in the second year. The rate of return being used in the appraisal is 8 per cent.

Consequent on this additional information the value of the net cash investment will be calculated as follows:

53

Net Cash Investment	£	£
Cost of new buildings and plant		
Year 1 £60 000+interest at 8 per cent		64 800
Year 0		65 000
		129 800
Net proceeds of sale of old plant		
Cash received	45 000	
Balancing charge, £8000 discounted for		
one year at 8 per cent (8000 × 0·926)	7 408	
		37 592
		92 208
Additional working capital*		25 000
Total		117 208

* If the working capital will be built up over two or more years, then the sums invested in Year 1 or later would need to be discounted.

Example 4.4

Porton Ltd are considering replacing their automatic packing machines. Expenditure on new plant will amount to £50 000. The machines to be replaced have a written down value for tax purposes of £5000, and are expected to realize £1500 on sale. The company operates in an area where the government provides a development grant towards new investment of 20 per cent of the cost (this is not likely to be received until the year following investment).

The criterion rate used by the company is 10 per cent after tax. The current tax rate is 50 per cent.

The net cash investment for Porton Ltd can be calculated as follows:

Net Cash Investment	£	£
Cost of new plant		50 000
Less Grant 20% of £50 000 discounted for one		
year at 10% (10 000 × 0·909)		9 090
		40 910
Sale of old plant		
Cash receivable	1500	
Additional capital allowances		
£5000−1500=£3500 at 50% discounted at		
10% (1750 × 0·909)	1591	
		3 091
		37 819

Example 4.5

Textron Ltd is to replace manual office work with book-keeping machines, and for this purpose is spending £8000.

In this case, the net cash investment will be the same as the book value, namely £8000. There are no machines to be replaced and no grant is receivable for this class of asset.

Annual Cash Flows

Under the heading of annual cash flows we are basically dealing with changes in the cash position of the business that result from the operations of the project. The segregation of the net cash investment outlined in the previous section of this chapter enables us to concentrate exclusively on the cash flows generated by operations unhindered by considerations relating to the acquisition of the assets.

The annual cash flows are made up of three basic components:

1. The increased revenue derived from the project due either to additional profits being earned or to cost savings made. Both factors will be before deduction of depreciation.
2. The tax payable on that increase in revenue.
3. The tax saved through the operation of the system of capital allowances or depreciation.

INCREASE IN REVENUE

An increase in the revenue of the business results in additional cash flowing into the business in each year when such an increase occurs. This increased cash flow will be the net result of a number of cash flows coming into the business and being paid out. Cash will be received continuously as a result of the sales made in respect of the new project, or cash outflows will be reduced by the operation of cost savings. Offset against this increment to the cash flows resulting from the project, may be outflows in respect of wages, materials, and overhead expenses. It will be noted that this applies only to actual cash outflows for overheads. Depreciation, although an overhead, involves no cash outflow, and is therefore excluded from the deductions that reduce the net value of the annual cash flows.

Unless in these components of the increased revenue there are exceptional items that require a different time phasing, the annual increments in profits as shown in the books of the business can be used as a measure of the value of the cash flows from this source. Normal differences in timing, such as the time taken to collect accounts from debtors, will be taken care of in calculating the net working capital included in the net cash investment.

The cash flow attributable to the increment in revenue can therefore be taken as the increase in net operating profits *before* depreciation and tax, which are attributable to the additional output or to the cost savings that result from the investment in the project.

TAXATION ON THE INCREASE IN REVENUE

The net amount of tax that will be payable on the increase in revenue from the project will be the net amount of two separate factors:

1. The tax due on the increase in income before depreciation.
2. The tax relief due to the operation of capital allowances.

Because of possible differences in the basis of computation and in the timing of their effects on the cash flows, it is usually best, in practice, to calculate these two components separately.

The tax liability on the increase in income reduces the cash flow arising from the operations of the project, the rate of tax payable depending upon whether the business is a corporation or an individual owner or partnership. The timing of the cash flow for the tax payment will be different from that of earning the increase in revenue. The actual time interval between these two events will depend upon the legal framework within which the business operates and the year-end date of the business.

For illustrative purposes, in subsequent examples it will be assumed that the tax is paid in the year following that in which the relevant profits were earned. This is only an assumption, and in practice the actual timing must be ascertained and used.

Capital Allowances

The acquisition of additional fixed assets enables the business to claim the benefit of capital allowances on those assets. The effect of these allowances will substantially reduce the final amount of tax payable. The benefit from these reliefs must be taken in the years in which they will be effectively received by the business.

The capital allowances will normally be set off against the taxable profits of the year in which the assets are *purchased*, therefore the effective receipt of the relief will occur in the year in which the tax on that year's profits would be payable. If, for example, assets are purchased in Year 0, and tax is payable a year after the related earnings, the relief for capital allowances would be received in Year 1.

It must be borne in mind that the cash benefit of capital allowances can be received only if there are profits against which the allowances can be offset. Where the business as a whole is making a loss, or just breaking even, the benefits from capital allowances must be deferred until such time as there are sufficient taxable profits against which they can be claimed.

Example 4.6

AB Ltd proposes to invest £20 000 in new machinery. The rate for first year allowances is 80 per cent. It is expected that the new machines will be replaced after six years. The increase in revenue (before depreciation) expected to result from the investment is as follows:

	£
Year 1	3000
Year 2	3200
Year 3	3200
Year 4	3500
Year 5	3500
Year 6	3300

The annual cash flows that would result from the project are as follows:

Year	Increase in revenue	Tax on increase in revenue at 50%	Capital allowances	Tax saved by capital allowances	Annual cash flow
	£	£	£	£	£
1	3 000	—	16 000	8 000	11 000
2	3 200	1 500	1 000	500	2 200
3	3 200	1 600	750	375	1 975
4	3 500	1 600	562	281	2 181
5	3 500	1 750	422	211	1 961
6	3 300	1 750	316	158	1 708
7	—	1 650	—	—	(1 650)
	19 700	9 850	19 050	9 525	19 375

The following points about the above calculations should be noted:

1. The tax payable on the increase in revenue is stepped down one year to allow for the time delay in payment.
2. It is assumed that the assets were purchased at such a time that the first year capital allowance would be given in Year 0. Due to the delay in paying the tax for that year, the cash flow benefit would not be received until Year 1.
3. Had the 100 per cent first year allowance been available the full £20 000 capital allowances could have been taken in Year 0 and benefited Year 1's cash flow.
4. A seventh year is added to the table to take care of the tax payment on the last year's operations.

5. It is assumed that the business as a whole has sufficient profits to absorb all the capital allowances as they become available.

6. The capital allowances for each year are computed as follows:

	£
Cost	20 000
Year 1 First Year Allowance 80%	16 000
	4 000
Year 2 Annual writing down allowance 25%	1 000
	3 000
Year 3 Annual writing down allowance 25%	750
	2 250
Year 4 Annual writing down allowance 25%	562
	1 688
Year 5 Annual writing down allowance 25%	422
	1 266
Year 6 Annual writing down allowance 25%	316
Written down value end of year 6	950

Residual Values

Each project will have an estimated life or time horizon, at the end of which the plant, buildings, working capital, etc., will be disposed of or put to other uses. Just as the project was charged with the net cash value of these investments when they were made, so it must now be credited with the funds that will be released by their disposal.

At the end of the life of the project we must appraise the flow of funds that will be created by the sale or disposal of the assets remaining in the project in order to give the appropriate credit to the project. As with other disposals of assets, there will be tax consequences that must be taken into account. Because of the difference in the basis of calculation it is useful to calculate these residual values separately from the annual cash flows.

FIXED ASSETS

When the fixed assets are to be sold or scrapped at the end of the life of the project, the starting point for the calculation of the residual cash flows is the cash expected to be received from their disposal. The sale value will be deducted from the 'pool' amount and thus reduce the future writing down allowances by this amount. If this amount exactly equals the notional written value for that asset, then there are no further tax consequences, the sale value having eliminated from the pool the exact amount that remains undepreciated for that asset.

If it is less, then a part of the undepreciated value remains in the pool and will continue to attract writing down allowances. For example, in the last illustration, if the asset was sold at the end of the sixth year for £200, there would be £750 left in the pool account that would continue to receive writing down allowances. Unless the amount is material, it will be found most convenient to assume that the whole of this difference is given as an additional capital allowance in the year of disposal or the year after.

If the amount received on sale exceeds the notional amount remaining in the pool for that asset, then the writing down allowances receivable in the future for other assets will be reduced by that amount. Again, referring to the previous example, if the amount received at the end of the sixth year was £1200, then this would reduce the pool value by £250 more than the asset's written down value and therefore reduce future allowances by that amount. It will be found most convenient to treat this as a drawback of capital allowances in the year of disposal or following year unless this treatment would make a significant difference to the result.

Where the asset was purchased prior to October 1970, these differences will emerge as straightforward balancing allowances or charges as shown on page 44.

If assets are likely to be retained in the business for other uses after the end of the project, then the amount the business would have received from their disposal should be taken into account. The reasoning behind this assertion is that the cash available to the business will be increased because, being available at that time, the asset reduces the need for the business to invest funds in buying a similar one for other uses. Although the answer is not so clear cut as in other cases, what we are looking for is the differential cash flows at the end of the life of the project. If there were no asset available from the project being wound up, then the business would have to purchase the item needed for the other use. This purchase would reduce the cash resources of the business. The fact that this item will be released from the project under consideration will then represent, in due course, a cash saving that is directly attributable to the project, and this must be taken into account. The measure of the cash flow for items so released but not sold will be the secondhand cash value in the market for a similar item of that age. If the item it will be used to replace can be identified at the first appraisal, then the actual cash saving by not having to purchase the other asset in the future should be included.

If the net cash investment has included provision for an increase in working capital, this increase will itself be released from the project when it comes to an end. There are no tax effects to consider in this case, and the figure to be used as the residual value for the item will be the same as the original investment unless there are losses on realization.

In some instances, a run-down of working capital investment may begin some time before the project finally comes to an end. In such cases, the release of funds caused by this run-down should be taken in the appropriate years during the life of the project.

TIMING OF RESIDUAL VALUES

As in other cases, the cash flows resulting from the residual values must be allocated to the years in which they are likely to be received. If some of the assets will be taken out of service and disposed of before the termination of the project, this must be recognized at the appropriate time. The remaining assets will normally be realized after the project has been closed down and, therefore, the year that will benefit from the resulting cash flows will be the year after the final operating year.

Should the cash value of capital allowance adjustments prove to be material, then it should be remembered that such values will not accrue for some time after the actual disposal. It will be appreciated that the time value of money will severely reduce the influence of cash flows for years ahead, which will be discounted by a high percentage factor. For example, an item receivable in twenty years' time at a 10 per cent rate of return has a present value factor of only 0·149, and a twenty-one years 0·135. The sum receivable must be substantial, in relation to the whole, for this to make a material difference.

In the examples in this book, it will be assumed that all residual values are received in the year following the closing down of the project.

Example 4.7

Lever and Co. Ltd are considering installing a conveyor belt system to reduce material handling in their plant. The details placed before the Board are as follows:

Cost   £10 000
Annual increase in revenue (before depreciation)   £3000
Life of plant   Eight years
Value of plant at end of eight years   £1000

Assume that the first year allowance is 60 per cent and the tax rate is 50 per cent. No increase in working capital is expected, and the company has adopted an 8 per cent criterion rate.

Does the project meet this minimum rate of return?

The appraisal, using the present value method, would proceed along the following lines:

1. *Net Cash Investment*   £

    Cost of conveyor system   10 000

2. *Annual and Residual Cash Flows*

Year	Increase in revenue	Tax on increase in revenue	Capital allowances	Tax saved by capital allowances	Cash flow	PV factor for 8%	Present value
	£	£	£	£	£	£	£
1	3 000	—	6 000	3 000	6 000	0·926	5 556
2	3 000	1 500	1 000	500	2 000	0·857	1 714
3	3 000	1 500	750	375	1 875	0·794	1 489
4	3 000	1 500	562	281	1 781	0·735	1 309
5	3 000	1 500	422	211	1 711	0·681	1 165
6	3 000	1 500	316	158	1 658	0·630	1 044
7	3 000	1 500	237	119	1 619	0·583	944
8	3 000	1 500	178	89	1 589	0·540	858
9	—	1 500	—	—	(1 500)	0·500	(750)
	24 000	12 000	9 465	4 733	16 733		13 329
Residual value Plant £1 000 *Less* drawback of capital allowances			(465)	(233)	767	0·500	383
			9 000	4 500	17 500		13 712

The total of the discounted cash flows at £13 712 exceeds the net cash investment of £10 000. The project therefore earns a rate of return greater than the criterion rate of 8 per cent, and would be an acceptable project.

The profitability index would be 13 712/10 000 = 1·37.

COMPARISON OF BOOK VALUES AND CASH FLOWS

The book values that would be taken into the accounts of Lever & Co. Ltd, in respect of the previous example would be directly related to the cash flows that have been used in the DCF calculation. While the timing of the items may differ, the cash flow has dealt with the same basic items. Table 4.1 shows a summary of the book values and the cash flows that illustrate this close relationship.

Example 4.8

The following report has been submitted to the Board of Directors of Leese Williams Ltd for consideration at their next board meeting:

'The condition of the boiler and power plant in Block C is causing concern because of frequent breakdowns and excessive maintenance costs. It is, over the next two years, proposed to renew the whole of the plant with modern labour saving equipment, which will also be more economical on fuel. The

TABLE 4.1, *Example 4.7. Comparison of Book Values and Cash Flows over the Life of the Project*

Totals used in cash flow		Totals recorded in the accounts	
	£		£
Net profit before		Profit:	
depreciation	24 000	Savings	24 000
Tax at 50%	12 000	Depreciation	
	12 000	(10 000–1 000)	9 000
Capital allowances £9 000			15 000
Tax at 50% on £9 000	4 500	Tax at 50%	7 500
	16 500	After tax profit	7 500
Cash receivable on sale		Cash flows shown by the	
of plant	1 000	accounts:	
		After tax profit	7 500
		Depreciation added back	9 000
		Proceeds from sale of	
		plant	1 000
	17 500		17 500

cost will be £50 000 spread equally over the two years. When fully installed the plant is expected to save £3000 per annum in running costs and £2000 in maintenance costs. The divisional management consider that the return of £5000 per annum on the cost of £50 000 to be adequate.'

The Board have asked the Finance Division to comment on the proposals, and, in particular, on whether the project would meet the criterion rate of return of 8 per cent after tax. On further examination of the project it is found that the written-down value for tax purposes of the existing plant is *nil*, and it is expected to yield £500 as scrap. The company will take advantage of the 100 per cent first year allowance. At the end of fifteen years it is expected that the new plant will have to be replaced and will have a scrap value at that time of £1500. The current tax rate is 50 per cent. As a criterion rate of return is given, the present value method can be used for this problem, and its solution would proceed along the following lines:

1. Net Cash Investment

Cost of new plant:	£	£
Year −1 £25 000+interest at 8%		
(25 000+2 000)		27 000
Year 0 £25 000		25 000
		52 000
Less realized on existing plant:		
Scrap value	500	
Less Balancing charge* of £500 at 50%	250	250
Total Net Cash Investment		51 750

2. Annual and Residual Cash Flows

Year	Cost saving	Tax on increase in revenue at 50%	Capital allow- ances†	Tax saved by capital allow- ances	Cash flow	P.V. factors for 8%	Present value
	£	£	£	£	£		£
1	5 000	—	50 000	25 000	30 000	0·926	27 780
2		2 500	—	—	2 500	0·857	
3			—	—	2 500	0·794	
4			—	—	2 500	0·735	
5			—	—	2 500	0·681	
6			—	—	2 500	0·630	
7			—	—	2 500	0·583	
8			—	—	2 500	0·540	=7·633
9			—	—	2 500	0·500	×£2 500 19 082
10			—	—	2 500	0·463	
11			—	—	2 500	0·429	
12			—	—	2 500	0·397	
13			—	—	2 500	0·368	
14			—	—	2 500	0·340	
15	5 000		—	—	2 500	0·315	
16	—	2 500	—	—	(2 500)	0·292	(730)
	75 000	37 500	50 000	25 000	62 500		46 132
16	Residual value Plant £1 500 Less drawback of capital allowances		(1 500)	(750)	750	0·292	219
			48 500	24 250	63 250		46 351

As the sum of the present values is less than the net cash investment, the project does not meet the minimum rate of return laid down by management, and on financial criteria alone would be rejected.

* Old plant assumed to be pre-1970.
† Some of these allowances might be claimable in Year −1 and therefore affect Year 0 cash flow.

It will be noted that in the last example the annual cash flows were the same for years 2 to 15. In this case, the calculations can be simplified by using the table of present value factors in Appendix B. The factor for £1 received *in each year* to fifteen years at 8 per cent is 8·559. Deduct from this the factor for Year 1 of 0·926 and we have the factor of 7·633 for £1 receivable for years 2 to 15. Only one calculation is then required to give the present value of those years' cash flows.

DIMINISHING INFLUENCE OF LATER YEARS

The annual cash flows and their related present value factors bring out quite clearly that the further we move into the future the less effect those values have on the result. At the same time, the longer the period of time over which the project stretches the more difficult it will be to forecast values for the later years. This uncertainty over values for years well into the future is therefore somewhat compensated for by the very reduced influence they will have on the final result. One advantage of using DCF is that it enables us to bring into account the cash flows for *all* the years and, at the same time, reduces the influence of those years which are the most difficult to forecast.

FINDING THE RATE OF RETURN BY INTERPOLATION

When using the rate of return method it is unlikely that the present values of the cash flows will give an exact rate of return. It is more likely that the rate will fall between two whole numbers. Assume that we are looking at a project that involves an investment of £10 000. Preliminary calculations show that, using the present value factors for 10 per cent, the present value total comes out at £9756. Using 8 per cent factors the present value totals £10 246. The rate lies between 8 and 10. To find the actual rate, take the difference between the two present values, and the difference between the present value for the lower rate and the net cash investment. The rate of return is then the lower rate plus the fraction of the interval between the two rates represented by these two differences. In the case given this would be $8+2(246/490)=9$ per cent.

Because of the uncertainties present in the values used, e.g., in forecasting increases in profits, there is no practical point in taking the result to decimal places. This would only be appropriate where the values had a high degree of certainty.

ALTERNATIVE LAYOUT

An illustration of an alternative layout for the DCF calculation is given in Table 4.3, the data used being the same as that in Example 4.8. It will be noted that this layout incorporates in the same statement the net cash investment and the annual and residual cash flows.

64

More than One DCF Solution

If the project being evaluated is one that involves future planned cash out-flows in respect of additions to capacity, etc., and these future cash flows are large enough to give a net outflow in those years, a pattern of cash flows similar to that given in Fig. 2.2 will emerge. In such a case more than a single rate of return may be found, a situation that would obviously detract considerably from the usefulness of DCF for investment appraisal.

This can be avoided by including planned additions to capacity in the net cash investment. Instead of including these cash outflows in the actual year in which they occur, we should follow the course previously advocated and include all the investment factors in the net cash investment. This will leave all future cash flows as positive values, with the exception of the final year when the tax payable on the last year's profit may exceed the residual values, or when there are cyclical patterns in the project that give sequences of positive and negative cash flows.

TABLE 4.2. *More than One Rate of Return*

1. *Project:* Investment £150.

  Cash flows—Year 1 £100, Year 2 £100, Year 3 £100, Year 4 £100,
      Year 5 —£270
  Cost of capital—8%

2. *Present Value of Cash Flows:*

Year	Cash flow	PV factor for 10%	Present value	PV factor for 26%	Present value
	£		£		£
1	100	0·909	91	0·794	79
2	100	0·826	83	0·630	63
3	100	0·751	75	0·500	50
4	100	0·683	68	0·397	40
5	(270)	0·621	(168)	0·315	(85)
			149		147

3. Bring back the negative cash flows year by year, at the cost of capital to the business, until a year is reached when the value is positive:

Year 5 —£270/1·08 = —£250+£100 Year 4= —£150 (value still negative)
Year 4 —£150/1·08 = —£139+£100 Year 3= —£39 (value still negative)
Year 3 —£39/1·08 = —£36+£100 Year 2=£64 (this is now a positive figure)

The DCF Calculation now appears as follows:

Year	Cash flow	PV factor for 7%	Present value
	£		£
1	100	0·935	94
2	64	0·873	56
			150

TABLE 4.3, Example 4.8. Alternative Layout of DCF Problem

Year	−1	0	1	2	3	4	5	6	7	8
Investment	(25 000)	(25 000)	—	—	—	—	—	—	—	—
Sale of Old Plant		250								
Operating inflow	—	—	5 000	5 000	5 000	5 000	5 000	5 000	5 000	5 000
Tax on above	—	—	—	(2 500)	(2 500)	(2 500)	(2 500)	(2 500)	(2 500)	(2 500)
Capital allowances	—	—	50 000	—	—	—	—	—	—	—
Tax saved by above	—	—	25 000	—	—	—	—	—	—	—
Residual value:										
Plant	—	—	—	—	—	—	—	—	—	—
Tax adjustment	—	—	—	—	—	—	—	—	—	—
Cash flow	(25 000)	(24 750)	30 000	2 500	2 500	2 500	2 500	2 500	2 500	2 500
PV factors for 8%	1·08	1·00	0·926	0·857	0·794	0·735	0·681	0·630	0·583	0·540
Present value	(27 000)	(24 750)	27 780	2 142	1 985	1 837	1 703	1 575	1 457	1 350

Year	9	10	11	12	13	14	15	16	Total
Investment	—	—	—	—	—	—	—	—	(50 000)
Sale of Old Plant									250
Operating inflow	5 000	5 000	5 000	5 000	5 000	5 000	5 000	—	75 000
Tax on above	(2 500)	(2 500)	(2 500)	(2 500)	(2 500)	(2 500)	(2 500)	(2 500)	(37 500)
Capital allowances	—	—	—	—	—	—	—	—	50 000
Tax saved by above	—	—	—	—	—	—	—	—	25 000
Residual value:									
Plant	—	—	—	—	—	—	—	1 500	1 500
Tax adjustment	—	—	—	—	—	—	—	(750)	(750)
Cash flow	2 500	2 500	2 500	2 500	2 500	2 500	2 500	(1 750)	13 500
PV factors for 8%	0·500	0·463	0·429	0·397	0·368	0·340	0·315	0·292	
Present value	1 250	1 157	1 073	992	920	850	788	(511)	(5 402)

If the problem cannot be resolved by including all investments in the net cash investment an alternative way of handling it is available. This involves taking the negative cash flow and discounting it back to the next preceding year at the cost of capital rate to the business. The discounted negative cash flow is then added to the cash flow for the preceding year. If the figure is positive, then proceed with the evaluation of the project in the normal way. If it is still negative, discount back a further year until a positive figure is arrived at. An illustration of the process is given in Table 4.2.

It must be emphasized that such situations are extremely rare and only when the negative cash flows are substantial is it likely to occur.

5 DCF Problems and Solutions

This chapter is devoted to the presentation of problems the reader can use to test his understanding of DCF methods. Model solutions are added. They are designed specifically to illustrate points that have been dealt with so far in the text, and should give a comprehensive view of the use of DCF in the context of capital investment appraisal. The methods of using the cash flows to arrive at the rate of return, or the present value when using a criterion rate of return, are given in chapter 2, and the factors that must be taken into account in arriving at the cash flows are given in chapter 4.

The author considers it imperative, if the essentials of DCF are to be fully grasped and the way the technique can be employed in practice fully understood, that practical work on realistic problems should be carried out. Even a few problems worked out conscientiously will materially assist in gaining an understanding of the meaning of the different items in DCF calculations, and how they are arrived at.

The model solutions are presented in the same way as that used in the illustrative examples. The author is not advocating the use of this method of presentation to the exclusion of all others. It is merely better, in a work of this kind, to conform to one style. When a systematic approach to the DCF solution has been achieved, the type of presentation any individual uses will be related to the problem being dealt with or the requirements of a particular firm.

STAGES IN THE SOLUTION

When appraising any capital investment problem by the DCF method, the principal purpose for which the technique is being used should always be borne in mind. That is, we shall be seeking an answer to the question, 'Will the cash flows resulting from an investment provide an adequate return on the funds locked up in that investment?'

There must be a definition of the net cash the firm is investing in the project and a definition of the cash flows that are to be compared with that investment. Discounting the different components of the investment and the cash flows in each year separately should be avoided, because difficulties will arise in determining what the investment is and what the returns are. This can lead to an inconclusive result. The return can be measured only by comparing the cash investment with the resulting cash flows, and priority should be given to the determination of these two factors.

When using the present value method the steps to be taken in arriving at a solution should be as follows:

1. There must be a management decision fixing the criterion rate, or rates, of return. A single rate may be used for all projects or different rates for different classes of project.

2. Determine the net cash investment with expenditures in years other than the base year brought to base year values. Netted against this cash outlay will be the cash value of receipts from the disposal of old plant, where this is appropriate, and any development or similar grants that will be received.

3. Estimate the cash flows that will result from the investment in each year of its life and allocate them to the years in which they will be received. These will include:
   (a) Earnings (excluding depreciation) resulting from the investment.
   (b) Tax payable on the increase in earnings.
   (c) Tax relief available through the operation of capital allowances.
   (d) Residual values at the end of the life of the project suitably adjusted for any tax consequences.

4. Find the present value of the future cash flows by discounting them at the criterion rate of return, using the tables in Appendix A or B.

5. When the sum of the present values of the future cash flows is greater than the net cash investment, the project gives a return greater than the criterion rate. When it is less than the net cash investment the project does not meet the criterion rate.

6. When the project return exceeds the criterion rate, calculate the profitability index so that projects can be ranked in order of profitability.

When using the rate of return method the steps to be followed in reaching a solution are as follows:

1. Calculate the net cash investment and annual cash flows as defined in 2 and 3 above.

2. Find a discounting rate that will reduce the value of the future cash flows to the value of the net cash investment. This rate is then the rate of return on the project.

3. The exact rate of return can be ascertained by interpolation.

69

Exercise 5.1

You are the office manager of BG Ltd and are in the process of submitting to your board a proposal for the installation of an accounting machine in your office at a cost of £2800. Until now, methods used in the office have been entirely manual. The new machine should produce cost savings (mainly clerical labour) of £500 per year. In order to justify this expenditure, you will be required to include in your submission to the board a note of the return that will be earned on this investment.

The machine is expected to have a life of eight years, after which it will have a residual value of £400. The current rate of tax is 40 per cent and 'Free depreciation' will be taken using up all the capital allowances in the first year.

1. *Net Cash Investment*
   Cost of machine   £2800

2. *Annual and Residual Cash Flows*

Year	Cost saving	Tax on cost saving	Capital allow-ances	Tax saving	Cash flow	PV factor for 10%	Present value
	£	£	£	£	£		£
1	500	—	2800	1120	1620	0·909	1473
2	500	200	—	—	300	0·826 ⎤	
3	500	200	—	—	300	0.751 ⎟	
4	500	200	—	—	300	0·683 ⎟	
5	500	200	—	—	300	0·621 ⎬ =4·426	1328
6	500	200	—	—	300	0·564 ⎟	
7	500	200	—	—	300	0·513 ⎟	
8	500	200	—	—	300	0·467 ⎦	
9	—	200	—	—	(200)	0·424	(85)
	4000	1600	2800	1120	3520		2716

Residual value £400
Less drawback of
capital allowances   (400)   (160)   240   0·424   102
                                       2400   960   3760   2818

The sum of the present values discounted at 10 per cent is almost exactly the same as the net cash investment, therefore the rate of return on the investment is 10 per cent *after tax*.

Comparison of Book Values and Cash Flows

Totals used in cash flows		Totals recorded in accounts	
	£		£
Increase in net profit		Profit:	
before depreciation	4000	Savings	4000
Tax at 40%	1600	Depreciation (2 800–400)	2400
	2400		1600
Capital allowances £2 400		Tax at 40%	640
Tax saving at 40%	960	Profit after tax	960
	3360	Cash flows shown by	
Cash receivable on		accounts:	
sale of plant	400	After tax profit	960
		Depreciation added back	2400
	3760	Proceeds from sale of	
		plant	400
			3760

Exercise 5.2

As a divisional manager of BG (France) you are formulating a proposal to put before your board to replace an existing kiln with a modern electric kiln. The present one has a written down value for tax purposes of Fr. 10 000 and is expected to yield Fr. 2000 on disposal. The new kiln will cost Fr. 80 000 exclusive of VAT and have an effective life of eight years, after which it is expected to realize Fr. 5000. The cost department has estimated that cost savings would amount to Fr. 24 000 per year.

Tax on companies (*impôt sur les sociétés*) is currently 50 per cent, and is assessed on a current year basis with four-fifths of the tax being paid on an estimated basis during the year. Depreciation allowances (*amortissement*) can be on a straight line or reducing balance basis. Using the latter method, the allowable rate would be 25 per cent. Where depreciable plant is disposed of, any gain or loss on the written down value is taken as a short-term capital gain or loss taxable at the normal rate.

The board expects all new investment to earn at least 8 per cent after tax, and requires divisional management to submit DCF calculations and a profitability index in support of its proposals.

1. *Net Cash Investment*	Fr.	Fr.
Cost of new kiln		80 000
Less Realized on sale of existing plant:		
Sale	2000	
Capital loss 10 000 − 2000 = 8000 × 50%	4000	
		6 000
		74 000

2. Annual and Residual Cash Flows

Year	Cost savings	Tax on cost savings	Deprecia-tion allowances	Tax saved	Cash flow	PV factors for 8%	Present value
	Fr.	Fr.	Fr.	Fr.	Fr.		Fr.
0	—	—	20 000	8 000	8 000	1·000	8 000
1	24 000	9 600	15 000	2 000 } 6 000 }	22 400	0·926	20 742
2	24 000	12 000	11 250	1 500 } 4 500 }	18 000	0·857	15 426
3	24 000	12 000	8 437	1 125 } 3 375 }	16 500	0·794	13 101
4	24 000	12 000	6 328	844 } 2 531 }	15 375	0·735	11 301
5	24 000	12 000	4 746	633 } 1 898 }	14 531	0·681	9 896
6	24 000	12 000	3 560	475 } 1 424 }	13 899	0·630	8 756
7	24 000	12 000	2 670	356 } 1 068 }	13 424	0·583	7 826
8	24 000	12 000	—	267	12 267	0·540	6 624
9	—	2 400	—	—	(2 400)	0·500	(1 200)
	192 000	96 000	71 991	35 996	131 996		100 472
Residual value Plant Fr. 5000 Capital loss allowable			3 009	1 504	6 504	0·500	3 252
			75 000	37 500	138 500		103 724

Note: Four-fifths of the tax is taken in the current year. It is assumed that the kiln is purchased in the tax year prior to its being put into use. On this basis, four-fifths of the benefit of depreciation allowances would be taken in Year 0 and one-fifth in Year 1. This pattern would be repeated throughout the period of depreciation.

The sum of the present values is greater than the net cash investment, therefore this project meets the minimum rate of return criterion. The profitability index for the project would be:

$$103\ 724/74\ 000 = 1·402$$

Exercise 5.3

You are preparing to take out a single premium life policy, the premium being £2000 net of tax reliefs. From the details that have been quoted to you, you have estimated that at the end of the fifteen years currency of the policy it would realize (including bonuses) the sum of £3600. Before committing yourself to this investment you would like to know the return

72

that would be earned, assuming that you survive the fifteen years, so that you can compare this with other forms of investment.

1. *Net Cash Investment* £2000

2. *Cash Flow*
In this case, there is a single cash flow of £3600 receivable after fifteen years. The PV factor that will reduce this to the net cash investment is 4 per cent, i.e., 3600×0.555 £1998

The rate of return to be earned would be 4 *per cent after tax.*

Exercise 5.4

(*a*) You have been asked to advise a company that has recently negotiated a licensing agreement with a US corporation that will enable it to manufacture and sell a new product as an addition to the company's existing product line. The manager of the new product line and his staff have been investigating the problems of manufacturing and selling the product with a view to obtaining board sanction for the necessary capital expenditure.

It is estimated that the product would sell at £6 per unit, and the variable costs associated with manufacture and sale would be £3 per unit. The new product would involve the company entering into commitments for additional fixed overheads of £50 000 per year (including £5000 p.a. depreciation). The sales volume is estimated at 20 000 units per year.

The company is situated in the London area and its existing buildings will be adequate to accommodate the new product. New plant and machinery will cost £60 000, and the additional working capital is estimated at £15 000. The foreseeable life for the product is twelve years, and at the end of that period the plant and machinery would have a scrap value of £1000. The current rate of corporation tax is 50 per cent.

The board requires a minimum rate of return on new investments of 10 per cent after tax.

1. *Net Cash Investment*	£	£
Cost of new plant		60 000
Additional working capital		15 000
Total		75 000

2. *Additional Annual Profits*		
Sales revenue £6 × 20 000		120 000
Less variable costs £3 × 20 000	60 000	
Fixed costs (exclude depreciation)	45 000	
		105 000
		15 000

3. Annual and Residual Cash Flows

Year	Increase in profit	Tax at 50%	Capital allow-ances	Tax saved	Cash flow	PV factors for 10%	Present value
	£	£	£	£	£		£
1	15 000	—	60 000	30 000	45 000	0·909	40 905
2	↑	7 500	—	—	7 500	0·826	
3		↑	—	—	7 500	0·751	
4			—	—	7 500	0·683	
5			—	—	7 500	0·621	
6			—	—	7 500	0·564	
7			—	—	7 500	0·513	=5·905 44 287
8			—	—	7 500	0·467	
9			—	—	7 500	0·424	
10			—	—	7 500	0·386	
11	↓		—	—	7 500	0·350	
12	15 000	↓	—	—	7 500	0·319	
13	—	7 500	—	—	(7 500)	0·290	(2 175)
	180 000	90 000	60 000	30 000	120 000		83 017

Residual value
Scrap value   1 000
Working capital 15 000
              16 000

		Capital allow-ances	Tax saved	Cash flow	PV factors	Present value
Less drawback of capital allowance		(1 000)	(500)	15 500	0·290	4 495
		59 000	29 500	135 500		87 512

The sum of the present values is greater than the net cash investment, therefore the project is acceptable. The profitability index is 87 512/75 000 = 1·17.

(b) The board have examined the proposals submitted to them and, in view of the lowness of the profitability index, have asked for a reappraisal of the project on the basis that the sales volume will reach only 18 000 units per year. At this level of turnover, the additional working capital required would only be £12 000.

1. *Net Cash Investment*

	£	£
Cost of new plant		60 000
Additional working capital		12 000
		72 000

2. *Additional Annual Profits*

	£	£
Sales revenue £6 × 18 000		108 000
Less variable costs—£3 × 18 000	54 000	
Fixed costs	45 000	
	—	99 000
Additional profits per year		9 000

3. *Annual and Residual Cash Flows*

Year	Increase in profit	Tax at 50%	Capital allow- ances	Tax saved	Cash flow	PV factor for 10%	Present value
	£	£	£	£	£	£	£
1	9 000	—	60 000	30 000	39 000	0·909	35 451
2	9 000	4 500	—	—	4 500	0·826	
3	9 000	4 500	—	—	4 500	0·751	
4	9 000	4 500	—	—	4 500	0·683	
5	9 000	4 500	—	—	4 500	0·621	
6	9 000	4 500	—	—	4 500	0·564	
7	9 000	4 500	—	—	4 500	0·513	5·905 26 573
8	9 000	4 500	—	—	4 500	0·467	
9	9 000	4 500	—	—	4 500	0·424	
10	9 000	4 500	—	—	4 500	0·386	
11	9 000	4 500	—	—	4 500	0·350	
12	9 000	4 500	—	—	4 500	0·319	
13	—	4 500	—	—	(4 500)	0·290	(1 305)
	108 000	54 000	60 000	30 000	84 000		60 719

Residual value
Plant 1 000
Working capital 12,000
13 000

Less drawback of

capital allowances			(1 000)	(500)	12 500	0·290	3 625
			59 000	29 500	96 500		64 344

The computation could have been shortened by discounting each element of the cash flows separately, viz.:

	£
Increase in profit £9000 p.a. Years 1–12 9000 × 6·814	61 326
Tax on increased profit £4500 p.a. Years 2–13 4500 × 6·194	(27 873)
Tax saving from capital allowances £30 000 × 0·909	27 270
Residual value £12 500 × 0·290	3 625
	64 348

In this case, the sum of the present values is less than the net cash investment and therefore the project would not be an acceptable one on these terms.

Exercise 5.5

The board of Forkson and Co. Ltd are considering launching a new product which they hope will restore the profitability of their company. In recent years, the company has only just broken even in trading with its existing products, and there is no immediate prospect that profitability can be restored on these lines.

The new product will involve the expenditure of £40 000 on new plant and machinery, and £10 000 on removal and re-training costs which will be refunded by a development grant. Writing down allowances of 25 per cent will be taken. It is estimated that the product will have a life of eight years, after which it will probably be replaced by a new line. The plant and machinery would be scrapped and should realize a scrap value of £6200. The increase in profit, excluding depreciation, expected from the new product is £10 000 per year. The new product would require the investment of some £9000 in working capital.

The current rate of tax is 50 per cent. What is the rate of return that is likely to be earned on the new product?

1. *Net Cash Investment*

	£
Cost of new plant and machinery and removal costs	50 000
Less Development Grant—£10 000 × 0·917	9 170
	40 830
Additional working capital	9 000
Total	49 830

2. *Annual and Residual Cash Flows*

Year	Increase in profit	Tax at 50%	Capital allow-ances	Tax saved	Cash flow	PV factors for 9%	Present value
	£	£	£	£	£		£
1	10 000	—	10 000	—†	10 000	0·917	9 170
2	10 000	5 000*	7 500	5 000†	10 000	0·842	8 420
3	10 000	5 000	5 625	3 750† ⎫ 1 250 ⎬	10 000	0·772	7 720
4	10 000	5 000	4 219	1 562 ⎫ 2 110 ⎬	8 672	0·708	6 140
5	10 000	5 000	3 164	1 582	6 582	0·650	4 278
6	10 000	5 000	2 373	1 187	6 187	0·596	3 688
7	10 000	5 000	1 780	890	5 890	0·547	3 222
8	10 000	5 000	1 335	667	5 667	0·502	2 845
9	—	5 000	—	—	(5 000)	0·460	(2 300)
	80 000	40 000	35 996	17 998	57 998		43 183

Residual value

Scrap	£6 200						
Working capital	9 000						
	15 200						
Less drawback of capital allowances		(2 196)		(1 098)	14 102	0·460	6 487
		33800		16 900	72 100		49 670

* It is assumed that the rest of the company just breaks even and the project profits and related tax are the only ones against which capital allowances can be offset.

† The benefit of the capital allowance and related tax saving is deferred until profits are available against which they can be relieved.

Exercise 5.6

A medium-sized spring-making company, STL Ltd, is proposing to expand its operations by purchasing an automatic coil-winding machine for £5000. Delivery of the new machine would take place half-way through the company's current year and it would contribute to that year's profits. An additional £1000 working capital would be required due to the expansion of business.

The machine is being acquired in an overseas territory whose government provides grants towards the cost of new investments at a rate of 45 per cent of that cost which is likely to be received in the year following acquisition. The balance of the cost is allowed in the form of a depreciation allowance of 20 per cent of the reducing balance.

The machine would be disposed of five years after the end of the current year, when it would have a secondhand value of £600. The increase in profits due to cost savings and additional business is expected to be £500 in the year in which the machine is installed, and £1200 in each subsequent year.

The company's criterion rate of return is 8 per cent after tax. The current tax rate is 40 per cent.

1. *Net Cash Investment*

	£
Cost of new machine	5000
Less Investment grant £2250 × 0·926	2083
	2917
Additional working capital	1000
Total	3917

2. *Annual and Residual Cash Flows*

Year	Increase in profit	Tax at 40%	Capital allowances	Tax saved	Cash flow	PV factors for 8%	Present value
	£	£	£	£	£		£
0	500	—	—	—	500	1·000	500
1	1200	200	550	220	1220	0·926	1130
2	1200	480	440	176	896	0·857	768
3	1200	480	352	141	861	0·794	684
4	1200	480	282	113	833	0·735	612
5	1200	480	225	90	810	0·681	552
6	—	480	180	72	(408)	0·630	(257)
	6500	2600	2029	812	4712		3989

Residual value

Machine	600
Working capital	1000
	1600

	Tax at 40%	Capital allowances	Tax saved	Cash flow	PV factors for 8%	Present value
Plus additional capital allowances		121	48	1648	0·630	1038
		2150	860	6360		5027

The sum of the present values is greater than the net cash investment and therefore the project would be acceptable. The profitability index for ranking purposes is $5027/3917 = 1.28$.

It will be noted in the above example that earnings from the project arose in the same year as that in which the asset was purchased. This means that the first year's earnings will fall in Year 0. It also means that, following the previous examples, the benefit from capital allowances will only be taken in Year 1.

Exercise 5.7

Capont Co. Ltd are currently considering the manufacture and sale of a new product, Brando, in order to supplement their existing product range. In order to put Brando on the market, an investment of £65 000 in plant and machinery would be required. In addition, there would be an increase in the value of working capital which is expected to amount to £19 000 in total, £14 000 of which would be needed in the year in which the other assets are acquired, and the remaining £5000 in the following year.

The new product is expected to increase profits before depreciation by £10 000 in the first year, £14 000 in each of the following seven years, £10 000 in the next two years, and £8000 in the final year, production and sales ceasing at the end of the eleventh year.

During the last year of the life of Brando (i.e., the eleventh year), £6000 of the working capital would be released as production runs down, the remaining £13 000 being released the following year. The plant and machinery would have a scrap value of £2900 after the eleventh year. Capital allowances will be provided at the 1972 UK rates and the board proposed to take advantage of the 100 per cent first year allowance.

The current rate of tax on profits is 50 per cent.

Capont Ltd makes a practice of calculating the rate of return on all new capital investment projects and selects those carrying the highest rates of return.

1. *Net Cash Investment*

	£	£
Cost of new plant and machinery		65 000
Working capital:		
Year 0 £14 000 × 1·000	14 000	
Year 1 £5000 × 0·917	4 585	
	——	18 585
Total		83 585

2. Annual and Residual Cash Flows

Year	Increase in profit	Tax at 50%	Capital allowances	Tax saved	Cash flow	PV factors for 9%	Present value
	£	£	£	£	£		£
1	10 000	—	65 000	32 500	42 500	0·917	38 972
2	14 000	5 000	—	—	9 000	0·842	7 578
3	14 000	7 000	—	—	7 000	0·772	5 404
4	14 000	7 000	—	—	7 000	0·708	4 956
5	14 000	7 000	—	—	7 000	0·650	4 550
6	14 000	7 000	—	—	7 000	0·596	4 172
7	14 000	7 000	—	—	7 000	0·547	3 829
8	14 000	7 000	—	—	7 000	0·502	3 514
9	10 000	7 000	—	—	3 000	0·460	1 380
10	10 000	5 000	—	—	5 000	0·422	2 110
11	8 000	5 000	—	—	3 000	0·388	1 164
12	—	4 000	—	—	(4 000)	0·356	(1 424)
	136 000	68 000	65 000	32 500	100 500		76 205
Residual values							
Working capital	6 000				6 000	0·388	2 328
Working capital	13 000						
Plant	2 900						
Less drawback of							
capital allowances			(2 900)	(1 450)	14 450	0·356	5 144
		62 100		31 050	120 950		83 677

The present value factors for 9 per cent reduces the value of the cash flows to almost the value of the net cash investment, therefore the rate of return is just over 9 per cent.

Exercise 5.8
A highway authority is evaluating the cost effectiveness of different types of highway construction. For new highways, varying types of construction can be used, each of which has a different initial cost level, and a different pattern of maintenance.

In considering its long-term commitments for both new construction and maintenance, the authority wishes to take into account the cost of the funds that are needed to finance the work.

The information that has been supplied to the authority by its consulting engineers regarding the possible cost levels for differing types of construction, and the consequent maintenance commitments are as follows:

		per route mile
Method A:	Initial cost	£350 000
	Maintenance costs every three years	£50 000
Method B:	Initial cost	£415 000
	Maintenance costs every five years	£52 000
Method C:	Initial cost	£482 000
	Maintenance costs every eight years	£55 000

The Treasurer's Department estimates the likely future costs of borrowing over the foreseeable future will be 6 per cent.

You have been asked to advise the authority, on the basis of the above information, the form of construction that would give the best return, taking into account the relative construction and maintenance costs, and the cost of borrowing. There is not expected to be any significant difference in the effective life of each method.

The solution to this problem can best be approached by considering the construction and maintenance costs as the total costs of the highway over its life. The method of construction with the lowest present value, using the cost of borrowing rate for the purpose of discounting, will be the one with the lowest overall cost.

Consideration must be given to the 'life' to be assigned for the purpose of evaluation. No terminal life is given in the data, and it must be assumed that the highway will be in operation for an indefinite period of time.

We know that the significance of future sums on the result diminishes the further away in time that they are. As a result, for our calculations, we can select a 'life' when the discounting effect becomes so high that future figures will not affect the result. In the solution below, a period of 40 years has been used for this purpose.

Using this basis, the next step is to discount at 6 per cent all the outlays associated with each method of construction.

1. *Construction Method A*

Year	Outlays	PV factor for 6%	Present value of outlays
	£		£
0	350 000	1·000	350 000
3	50 000	0·840	
6	50 000	0·705	
9	50 000	0·592	
12	50 000	0·497	
15	50 000	0·417	
18	50 000	0·350	
21	50 000	0·294	Total = 4·695 234 750
24	50 000	0·247	
27	50 000	0·207	
30	50 000	0·174	
33	50 000	0·146	
36	50 000	0·123	
39	50 000	0·103	
Total	1 000 000		584 750

2. Construction Method B

Year	Outlays	PV factor for 6%		Present value of outlays
	£			£
0	415 000	1·000		415 000
5	52 000	0·747		
10	52 000	0·558		
15	52 000	0·417		
20	52 000	0·312	Total =	138 736
25	52 000	0·233	2·668	
30	52 000	0·174		
35	52 000	0·130		
40	52 000	0·097		
Total	831 000			553 736

3. Construction Method C

Year	Outlays	PV factor for 6%		Present value of outlays
	£			£
0	482 000	1·000		482 000
8	55 000	0·627		
16	55 000	0·394		
24	55 000	0·247	= 1·520	83 600
32	55 000	0·155		
40	55 000	0·097		
Total	£757 000			565 600

From the point of view of the highway authority, Method B would be the most advantageous, since it has the lowest present value of costs. The above analysis might well be expanded, however, to take into account differences in social costs due to the varying frequency and duration of the road being wholly or partially out of service. This could well be incorporated into the calculations previously made if the data are available.

6 Alternative Choice Problems and Leasing versus Buying

Once a decision that a project is a worthwhile investment has been made, management may well want to consider two further aspects before finally authorizing the project. One aspect concerns the examination of alternative methods of carrying out the purposes of the project, in order to see if higher rates of return are provided by the method originally discussed. The other aspect is a quasi-financial one, to discover whether it would be advantageous for the business to own the assets incorporated in a project, or merely to acquire the use of the assets without ownership, through the medium of leasing. The first part of this chapter will be concerned with the handling of alternatives generally, and the second part will deal with a specialized choice problem, that of leasing versus buying.

Alternative Choice Problems

IMPORTANCE OF SEEKING ALTERNATIVES

The uncritical acceptance by management of the projects that are put up to them for approval, even when those projects meet the minimum rate of return criterion, can be a significant factor in keeping the return on capital employed at a lower rate than might otherwise be the case. The management that is fully alive to the effect the rate of return has on the general level of profitability of its company will be in continuous search for alternative ways of achieving the objectives that will raise the general level of profitability of the firm. This can be done most easily before the project is approved and funds actually committed, and it entails the fullest examination of projects before they are approved, including a comprehensive search for more profitable alternatives.

The funds available to the business must, in most cases, be looked upon as a scarce resource from which the maximum benefit must be derived. Each proposal to appropriate funds for a particular purpose must be regarded in this light. The allocation of funds to one purpose necessarily means that alternative and competing projects cannot be proceeded with. The cost of any project is then, in a sense, the return that could have been

82

earned on those competing projects had they not been dropped in favour of the initial proposal.

In any investment project, the basic elements that affect the rate of return that can be earned, and that should receive the most serious consideration from the managers concerned are:

1. The volume of funds invested.
2. The increase in income arising from the project.
3. The differential tax effects.

The successful management will be the one that consistently selects the right combination of these factors and so produces a higher than average rate of return. It will be achieved only by searching for the optimum combination of these factors in each project. Usually, it will be much easier to alter the balance of a project before any investment is made and funds become locked up in other forms of assets than it will be to try to improve the profitability of a project, once it is running, by means of cost reduction programmes, value analysis, and so on. This is not to decry these techniques or to deny their importance in keeping the business profitable. Indeed, they have a vital role to play in this sphere, but the essential thing is that each project should be launched in such a way that it combines the resources used in the best possible way and makes the most profitable use of the funds of the business. A healthy infant stands a much better chance of becoming a virile adult than a weakling, and a project should be launched in the healthiest state.

Economy in the Use of Funds
Economy in the use of funds will materially assist in achieving a maximum return on capital employed. The investment of £20 000 on a project that will produce an operating profit of £4000 is likely to be much more profitable than an investment of £35 000 on a more sophisticated version of the same project that will produce an operating profit of £5500. The investment of £35 000, considered on its own, may well satisfy the minimum rate of return required and, as such, be accepted by management. If, however, management is made aware of an alternative that requires an investment of only £20 000, it will concentrate attention on the basic problem, which is, whether or not the incremental investment of £15 000 in the more sophisticated version of the project will provide a return comparable to what could be earned by investing that sum in other projects.

When there is more than one alternative for a particular project, each of which requires the investment of different amounts, management must be in a position to evaluate the different levels of investment in order to determine the return on each incremental sum involved.

In the case of the alternatives already cited, management would want to know, not only the return on the initial proposal to invest £20 000, but also what the return would be on the *additional* investment of £15 000 in a more sophisticated version of the project. It is the return on this increment in the investment that will determine whether the £35 000 version of the project will be approved, or the smaller project.

If this investment of an additional £15 000 in the initial project, and the consequent increase in the income of £1500, provide a rate of return that is more than what can be earned in other projects, then the larger version of the project would be approved. If, however, the return proves to be less than could be earned elsewhere, then the smaller version would be the one approved.

From our examination of capital investment appraisal, we have seen that it is not the absolute level of profits that is relevant to an investment decision, but the level of profits related to the volume of funds invested. In many cases, however, the level of management that originates investment proposals may have a natural tendency to examine the project only from the point of view of producing the maximum level of profits for the area of the business they happen to control. This will often result in the investment proposal being framed in such a way as to bring the greatest increase in *profit* to their section of the business rather than the highest *profitability*.

This is a process that senior management must watch with great care. They must always have the profitability of the business as a whole as their first consideration, and their examination of an investment project should take into account other ways of carrying it out. Deliberately, or otherwise, this element of choice may not be readily apparent in the proposals before them.

Economy in the use of funds does not necessarily mean that one is only looking for ways of *reducing* the funds invested in a project. The advantages of large-scale automation may drastically affect the cost structure of a business. When projects are in the planning stage is the time to decide whether or not an injection of additional funds into the project to provide more advanced automated equipment, or to carry operations on to a higher scale (e.g., in the chemical industry), will produce a more than commensurate return on the additional funds involved.

Operating Profitability
The way in which the operations of the business are carried out may offer considerable elements of choice. The particular types of materials, methods of machining, layout of plant, degree of sub-contract, and so on, are all matters that should be carefully investigated at this stage. Once the commitment to particular machinery, to a specified layout, etc., has been made, the element of choice open to managerial decision has been greatly restricted. The planning stage is the time when painless adjustments to the original plan can be made, if investigations reveal that this is desirable.

Tax Considerations

Tax considerations should not be omitted in the search for alternative combinations of factors for carrying out a project. Within the United Kingdom, there are discriminatory elements between different areas of the same country, as in Britain's development grant system, these may have significant effects on the return that can be earned by a project. Such savings should be weighed up and balanced against any possible increases in costs that would arise through operating in a different geographical area.

Outside the United Kingdom, the Republic of Ireland offers significant tax exemptions for new businesses set up there. The increasing internationalization of business will mean that, more and more, management will take into account and estimate the effects of operating in different countries. This trend will be reinforced by Britain's entry into the Common Market.

Approach to Alternative Choice Problems

Problems involving alternative choice should not be approached haphazardly but should follow logical lines. The volume of work can be substantially reduced by discarding at an early stage those alternatives that, from the evidence, cannot be as profitable as other propositions. This type of elimination may be carried out by using normal forecasting techniques during preparation of the basic data. Once the clearly unprofitable alternatives are eliminated, those remaining must be arranged in a logical sequence.

A useful scheme for solving multiple choice problems is given below. This sequence starts, as should all our thinking, with a serious appraisal of the object of the investment and what it is trying to achieve.

1. Analyse and define the objective of the proposal.
2. Set out the possible alternative methods of achieving that objective.
3. Drop any alternatives which, on the data already assembled, are non-starters.
4. Quantify all the consequences that will flow from each of the remaining alternatives.
5. Some of the consequences of alternatives may not be capable of being quantified, e.g., employee relationships. These must be evaluated in some way and taken into account in the final decision.
6. Weigh up all the factors in 4 and 5 for each alternative, and reach a decision.

NON-FINANCIAL DATA

It will be noted that in the above scheme, mention has been made of factors that cannot be evaluated in financial terms. This is common to most of the decisions taken in the field of business, and it is referred to here as an additional reminder that, normally, decisions should not be taken on financial criteria alone. The non-financial effects of an investment decision may have far-reaching results that cannot be measured in monetary terms, and it would be quite wrong to insist that any decision of the type dealt with in this book should be made as though the financial area of the business operated in a vacuum.

Obviously, non-financial data cannot be incorporated in the DCF solution, but this does not mean they should be ignored at the decision-taking stage. The attitude that insists that financial data are the sole criteria on which decisions should be made is sometimes found, but it should be guarded against and, in the decision-making process, adequate weight given to non-financial data.

Sequential Treatment of Alternatives

Once alternatives that are to be evaluated have been defined, the next step is to quantify the consequences of each course of action that is to be considered. Each of the alternatives can be evaluated as though it were a separate project without any reference to the other alternatives, and then the one that shows the highest rate of return selected. But, as has already been demonstrated, this might not be the best solution. The important factor, as far as management is concerned, is the return on the *incremental* investment of funds as between one alternative and another. By taking a step by step progression through all the alternatives that are to be appraised, starting with that with the lowest cash investment, it is possible to estimate the return that will be earned on each additional 'slice' of funds.

Essentially, all DCF problems involve a choice between alternatives, even if that choice lies between carrying out a project or doing nothing. To do nothing is as much a choice as any other decision, and this has been recognized in the problems dealt with so far. Until now we have been comparing the project with the existing conditions and we have carried out our appraisal by examining the incremental cash flows relative to each. Now we shall proceed one step further and compare the incremental cash flows between a series of alternatives for the same project.

The difference in treatment of the various elements of the cash flow in this comparison and the approach necessary in dealing with particular difficulties encountered is illustrated in the following example.

Example 6.1

The directors of Rose and Co. Ltd are considering the renewal or replacement of the power plant of their main factory. This plant is fifteen years old and it is proposed that it should undergo modification together with the installation of automated controls at a cost of £10 000. When complete, the work should result in cost savings of the order of £2000 per annum. The written-down value of the plant for tax purposes is £3000, and if it were to be sold now it would realize approximately £500 as scrap. The renovation would give the plant a further useful life of ten years, at the end of which it would realize about the same amount as scrap.

After looking at the scheme in some detail, a further proposal has been formulated that would involve complete replacement of the power plant by one incorporating all the latest fuel-saving devices. This would cost £25 000 and would result in cost savings of £4000 per year. It would have a useful life of fifteen years, at the end of which it would realize £700 as scrap.

Accelerated capital allowances of 60 per cent in the year of purchase and writing down allowances of 25 per cent in subsequent years would be available.

STAGE 1

The first step in solving the problem is to decide whether the less expensive alternative in terms of cash outlay would be a project that would qualify under the criterion rate of return. This part of the solution will proceed along lines used in previous examples.

1. *Net Cash Investment* £

    Cost   10 000

2. *Annual and Residual Cash Flows*

Year	Cost saving £	Tax on cost saving £	Capital allowances £	Tax saved £	Cash flow £	PV factors for 10%	Present value £
1	2 000	—	6 000	3 000	5 000	0·909	4 545
2	↑	1 000	1 000	500	1 500	0·826	1 239
3		↑	750	375	1 375	0·751	1 035
4			562	281	1 281	0·683	875
5			397	199	1 199	0·621	745
6			298	149	1 149	0·564	648
7			224	112	1 112	0·513	570
8			167	83	1 083	0·467	506
9	↓		125	63	1 063	0·424	451
10	2 000	↓	94	47	1 047	0·386	408
11	—	1 000	—	—	(1 000)	0·350	(350)
	20 000	10 000	9 617	4 809	14 809		10 672

Residual value
Scrap value of plant £500
Less drawback of capital

allowances			(117)	(59)	441	0·350	154
			9 500	4 750	15 250		10 826

87

The sum of the present value of the cash flows is greater than the net cash investment, therefore the project meets the minimum rate of return requirements.

STAGE 2

The appraisal of the alternative with the lower cash investment has shown that this would be an acceptable project. We must now turn our attention to the appraisal of the return that would be earned by investing the additional funds required to install the completely new plant. Here we shall be trying to decide whether the *additional* net cash investment will provide *additional* cash flows sufficient to give a return of more than 10 per cent.

Net Cash Investment (Additional cash required to install new power plant.) The net cash investment here will be the difference between the cash outlay that would be involved in each of the alternatives. This can be ascertained by first calculating the cash investment required for the new plant and deducting from this figure the cash investment required for the renovation proposal dealt with above.

	£
Cost of new power plant	25 000
Less sale of old plant—	
Scrap value	500
(Drawback of capital allowances offset against capital allowances for new plant)	
	24 500
Less cost of modifying existing plant as detailed in Stage 1	10 000
Additional cash outlay through completely replacing plant instead of modifying it	14 500

Annual and Residual Cash Flows

The first step in calculating the annual and residual values is to detail the differences that exist in the component items as between completely replacing and merely modifying the plant:

1. *Increase in Income.* The difference between the increase in income under each of the alternatives is £4000−£2000=£2000.

2. *Capital Allowances.* The tax saving in respect of capital allowances is based upon the difference between the capital allowances for each alternative:

		New Plant			
Year	Modified Plant	Capital allowances on new plant	Drawback of capital allowances on replaced plant	Net	Difference
	£	£	£	£	£
1	6 000	15 000	625	14 375	8 375
2	1 000	2 500	469	2 031	1 031
3	750	1 875	351	1 524	774
4	562	1 406	264	1 142	580
5	397	1 055	198	857	460
6	298	791	148	643	345
7	224	593	111	482	258
8	167	445	83	362	195
9	125	334	63	271	146
10	94	250	47	203	109
	9 617	24 249	2 359	21 890	12 273

Remaining allowances included in
£4 000 net of tax value at end of
year 10 (See 3 below)

3. *Life and Residual Value.* In the example, each of the alternatives has a different timespan or horizon. This is frequently a feature when a number of alternative courses of action has to be examined. The modification proposal has a life of ten years and the completely new plant has a life of fifteen years, thus we cannot compare the full lives of both projects since, beyond the time period covered by the shorter life, there is no basis for comparison. If we were to try to calculate the cash flows beyond the period of ten years what basis could be used? Logically, the savings resulting from the installation of the new plant would have to be compared with the savings from the equipment that will replace the modified plant after it is scrapped at the end of ten years. This factor is unknown at this stage and, in fact, might well result in negative cash flows if it were. In ten years' time plant may be much more efficient than existing designs.

The restriction of the time horizon to the shortest life does not mean that the value of the cash flows after that period must be ignored altogether. At the end of ten years the new plant will have a much higher value to the business than its final residual value because of the five years' life remaining. The procedure in such cases is to calculate or estimate the value of the plant to the business at the end of the time horizon for the DCF calculation. This will place the alternatives on a comparable basis.

If we assume that the directors consider that the new plant at the end of ten years would have a value to the business of £4000 net of tax effect, the difference between the alternatives for the residual value at the end of ten years would be as follows:

New Plant   £
   Residual value   4000 net of tax
Modified plant
   Residual value calculated as for Stage 1   441

Difference in residual values after ten years   3559

Having evaluated the differences for the components of the DCF calculation, we can now proceed to compare the alternatives within the normal
DCF framework as shown in Table 6.1.

TABLE 6.1, *Example 6.1. Evaluation of the Incremental*
Annual and Residual Values at the Criterion Rate

Year	Increase in income	Tax at 50%	Capital allowances	Tax saved	Cash flow	PV factors for 10%	Present value
	£	£	£	£	£		£
1	2 000	—	8 375	4 187	6 187	0·909	5 624
2	↑	1 000	1 031	516	1 516	0·826	1 252
3	│	↑	774	387	1 387	0·751	1 042
4	│	│	580	290	1 290	0·683	881
5	│	│	460	230	1 230	0·621	764
6	│	│	345	172	1 172	0·564	661
7	│	│	258	129	1 129	0·513	579
8	│	│	195	98	1 098	0·467	513
9	│	│	146	73	1 073	0·424	455
10	2 000	↓	109	54	1 054	0·386	407
11	—	1 000	—	—	(1 000)	0·350	(350)
	20 000	10 000	12 273	6 136	16 136		11 828
Residual value					3 559	0·350	1 246
					19 695		13 074

The sum of the present values in Table 6.1 is £13 074 compares with an
incremental net cash investment of less than £15 000. This indicates that the
rate of return on this incremental slice of investment is less than the criterion
rate.

SUMMARY

The general approach to multiple choice problems can be summarized as
follows:

1. Evaluate the incremental investment and returns for each alternative.
2. Select the alternative showing the lowest net cash investment and use
   this as the basis for a normal project evaluation by DCF, at this stage
   ignoring other alternatives.
3. If this does not meet the minimum standards for projects, abandon
   this alternative and repeat for the next alternative, i.e., that with the
   next highest cash investment.

4. When an alternative is found which, on the usual project evaluation, would provide a basis for approval, this alternative is compared with the alternative with the next highest cash investment to measure the return on the increase in investment.

5. This process is repeated until all alternatives have been compared.

Leasing Versus Buying

The development of leasing facilities provides management with an acceptable method of acquiring the *use* of fixed and other assets without necessitating the outlay of funds for their purchase. Whether or not management will use the leasing facilities available as a means of easing their capital requirements will depend upon a number of factors other than the rate of return involved.

The leasing decision, unlike the problems that have been dealt with so far, may have far-reaching effects upon the balance sheet figures for the business. Leased assets do not appear in the balance sheet since the assets are not owned. This may have repercussions on the ability of the business to raise further funds by borrowing, since the business will have fewer assets that could be charged as a security. The rentals payable will reduce the earnings of the business and restrict the earnings cover for interest and dividends. In the long run, such factors may also affect the share value, as effectively they are introducing a further element of gearing into the company. Leasing decision is not, therefore, a straightforward DCF problem but one with much wider financial implications.*

Management might not have any choice. Shortage of funds can mean that leasing is the only way to acquire the use of the asset. On the other hand, lenders of money, in order to protect the asset backing for their loans, may prohibit either expressly or implicitly the use of leasing. Where, however, there is a choice open to management, DCF should be used to establish which of them is preferable. This appraisal is an extension of the multiple choice problem, but it is treated separately because of other financial considerations.

In this case, after it has taken the initial decision that a project should be proceeded with, management moves on to a further decision as to whether or not the assets should be leased. Leasing an asset requires no investment of funds. Instead, the business disburses a series of payments that stretches into the years ahead, in the form of rentals. On the other hand, the outright purchase of an asset requires the outlay of cash at the time of purchase without any liability for further payment in the future. Management will therefore want an answer to the question: 'If we commit the funds necessary to buy the assets will this produce enough savings in future years, i.e., by not

* See 'A New Look at Leasing', M. G. Wright, *The Accountant*, 16 January 1965, pages 60–3.

having to pay rentals, to produce a high enough return to qualify for inclusion in the capital budget?'

The purchase of an asset that might otherwise be leased will absorb funds that could have been used for investment in other areas of the business. The commitment of funds in this case should be able to earn more, as compared with leasing the assets, than the funds could earn, if used for these other purposes. In other words, we are looking at the opportunity costs of the capital concerned, and the cost of the funds will effectively be the return they could earn in the business in other uses.

This approach is implicit in other investment decisions, since the allocation of funds in any year will involve ranking projects in such a way that none of the projects rejected will have a rate of return that is higher than the projects that are approved (after allowing for differences in risk, etc.).

This factor is highlighted here so that it will be fully understood that the lease decision is not dependent on the cost of the funds to the business except in so far as they set a lower limit to the return that would be acceptable. The criterion that must be taken into account in making the decision is the return that could be earned on competing projects.

The leasing decision can be brought into the general capital investment appraisal system by defining the cash outlay that would be involved if the assets are purchased, and comparing this with the increase in the annual and residual cash flows that would result from that decision. This approach would place the leasing decision on the same basis as other investment decisions, and allows it to be ranked in the same way as other projects.

Steps in the Solution of Leasing Problems
The logical sequence of steps to be taken in solving a leasing problem can be set out as follows:

1. Assess the project on the basis that the assets are purchased to see whether it is a project that would qualify for approval under the normal rules.
2. If the project does qualify, then calculate the net cash investment necessary to purchase the assets as against leasing them.
3. Calculate the incremental cash flows that would arise as between leasing and buying.
4. Calculate the rate of return, or profitability index, represented by the relationship between 2 and 3 above.

Example 6.2
Cracken & Co. Ltd is considering a project that involves the purchase of a machine for £30 000 which would have a life of six years with no residual

value at the end of that period. The machine would produce cost savings of £9400 a year and would be eligible for accelerated capital allowances of 60 per cent and writing down allowances of 25 per cent.

As a result of further inquiries, it has been established that the company could rent the machine at £7500 per annum for six years certain, after which it could be retained at a nominal rental.

The company can earn at least 11 per cent after tax in other areas of the business. The tax rate is 50 per cent.

STAGE 1. EVALUATION OF THE PROJECT

The first step in solving the problem set out in Example 6.2 is to appraise the project in the normal way. The data for this appraisal is set out in Table 6.2. From the results given in the table it can be seen that the rate of

TABLE 6.2, *Example 6.2. Evaluation of the Project on a normal DCF Basis*

1. *Net Cash Investment*

	£
Cost of Machine	30 000

2. *Annual and Residual Cash Flows*

Year	Cost savings	Tax at 50%	Capital allowances	Tax saved	Cash flow	PV factors for 17%	Present value
	£	£	£	£	£		£
1	9 400	—	18 000	9 000	18 400	0·855	15 732
2	9 400	4 700	3 000	1 500	6 200	0·731	4 532
3	9 400	4 700	2 250	1 125	5 825	0·624	3 635
4	9 400	4 700	1 687	843	5 543	0·534	2 960
5	9 400	4 700	1 266	633	5 333	0·456	2 432
6	9 400	4 700	949	475	5 175	0·390	2 018
7	—	4 700	—	—	(4 700)	0·333	(1 565)
	56 400	28 200	27 152	13 576	41 776		29 744
Residual value	Nil						
Plus additional							
capital allowances			2 848	1 424	1 424	0·333	474
			30 000	15 000	43 200		30 218

return on the project is a little in excess of 17 per cent (the actual rate would be approximately 17·4 per cent). On the basis of comparable rates of return in other parts of the business this is a project that would be approved by management.

As there is an opportunity in connection with this project to rent the machine, the next stage in the evaluation is to see whether it would be better to lease the machine or to buy it.

STAGE 2. THE LEASE OR BUY DECISION

At this stage, the first step is to determine the incremental cash flow for the investment and the annual and residual cash flows.

Net Cash Investment. The leasing alternative will require no outlay of funds, whereas the purchase of the machine will. In the case under review, there is no value of replaced plant to consider, the treatment of which will be dealt with later. The incremental net cash investment will therefore be the same amount as was used in Stage 1, namely, £30 000.

Annual and Residual Cash Flows. To determine the incremental cash flows, we must examine and compare the cash flows and tax implications of the alternatives. If the machine is purchased, the business will not incur the annual lease payments of £7500 per annum. This saving will increase the taxable profits of the business and the cash flow will be adjusted for this in the normal way, the tax payments being allocated to the appropriate years. The cash flows in respect of the net saving of rental would then appear as follows:

Year	Rental saved	Tax on rental savings	Net cash savings
	£	£	£
1	7500	—	7500
2	7500	3750	3750
3	7500	3750	3750
4	7500	3750	3750
5	7500	3750	3750
6	7500	3750	3750
7	—	3750	(3750)

If the machine is purchased, the company will also be entitled to the benefits from the capital allowances, whereas if it is leased the benefit from the allowances will accrue to the leasing company, who are the owners of the machine. There will, therefore, be an increase in the cash flows if the asset is purchased, which is attributable to the cash value of these allowances. These values will be the same as those used in the Stage 1 calculation. In addition, the business that owns the asset will benefit from any residual values that may be present at the end of the life of the project. Again, these would not be present were the asset to be leased.

The annual and residual cash flows will therefore be made up of the following three factors:

1. The net savings on rentals.
2. The cash value of the capital allowances.
3. Any residual value.

These factors follow the pattern of the normal DCF calculation, and we can now bring them together to calculate the cash flows for each year and arrive at the rate of return earned in the normal way. The data for Example 6.2 are shown in Table 6.3.

In Table 6.3 the present values of the cash flows after using a 10 per cent

94

discount factor total almost the same amount as the net cash investment. This means that the rate of return earned by buying the asset rather than leasing it would be 10 per cent. Other uses of funds in the business can earn a rate of return of 11 per cent, therefore it would pay the business to lease the asset and use the funds in other areas of the business where the higher rate can be achieved.

TABLE 6.3, *Example 6.2. Evaluation of the Lease or Buy Decision*

1. *Net Cash Investment*
   Value as given in Stage 1   £30 000

2. *Annual and Residual Cash Flows*

Year	Rental Saved	Tax on saving at 50%	Capital allow-ances	Tax saved	Cash flow	PV factors for 10%	Present value
	£	£	£	£	£		£
1	7 500	—	18 000	9 000	16 500	0·909	14 998
2	7 500	3 750	3 000	1 500	5 250	0·826	4 337
3	7 500	3 750	2 250	1 125	4 875	0·751	3 661
4	7 500	3 750	1 687	843	4 593	0·683	3 137
5	7 500	3 750	1 266	633	4 383	0·621	2 722
6	7 500	3 750	949	475	4 225	0·564	2 383
7	—	3 750	—	—	(3 750)	0·513	(1 924)
	45 000	22 500	27 152	13 576	36 076		29 314
Residual value Nil *Plus* additional capital allowances			2 848	1 424	1 424	0·513	730
			30 000	15 000	37 500		30 044

Net Cash Investment in the Leasing Decision

In the Example 6.2, the same value for the net cash investment was used for both the original project evaluation and the leasing decision. This was because in both cases no consideration had to be given to the cash value of plant that would be replaced by the new project. Where this is not the case the treatment of residual values of replaced plant will differ as between the evaluation of the project as a whole and that of the leasing decision.

In the treatment of the project as a whole, the cash value of plant that is being replaced will be used to reduce the amount of the net cash investment. This is correct in the context of that decision, since we are measuring the amount by which the cash resources of the business will be depleted as a result of that decision.

When, however, we turn to the leasing decision, the situation is quite different. The determination of the cash outflow due to the purchase of the plant rather than leasing it, involves comparing the cash flows associated with acquiring the use of the plant under each of the alternatives. In this case *both* the alternatives provide for the replacement of the existing plant and, therefore, the inflow of funds from the disposal of the replaced plant will be common to both alternatives and will not affect the incremental cash flow, the net cash investment being the net cost of purchasing the plant.

Let us assume that Machine A is to be replaced by a new machine. The net realizable value of A is £200 and the net cost (after any grants, etc.) of the new machine is £1200. Therefore:

1. The net cash investment for the project decision as a whole will be £1200−200=£1000. This is the net cash outlay involved in replacing one machine with another.
2. The net cash outlay associated with the decision between leasing and buying can be summarized as follows:

	Machine Leased £	Machine Purchased £
Cash from disposal of old machine	+200	+200
Purchase price of new machine	—	−1200
Net cash movement	+200	−1000

The net cash outlay differential between the alternatives is therefore the difference between −£1000 and +£200, or £1200, which is the same amount as the net cost of the new machine.

Example 6.3

MO Transport Ltd is considering replacing its fleet of trucks (ten in all), each of which has an estimated realizable value, net of tax effects of £100. The new trucks would cost £1000 each ready for service, and after three years it is expected they would be replaced and at that time have a second-hand value of £400 each. The savings expected from reduced running costs by having new vehicles is put at £250 per vehicle per year.

A leasing company has approached MO Transport and offered to lease the trucks to the company, already painted in its livery, for the sum of £620 per vehicle for each of three years. In addition, the leasing company will pay the road fund licence and maintain the vehicles. It is estimated that the annual road tax is £50 per vehicle and the maintenance cost £180 per vehicle each year.

The criterion rate of return for the company is 8 per cent.

The appraisal of the replacement decision is shown in Table 6.4. As the present value of the cash flows is marginally higher than the net cash investment the decision is likely to be in favour of replacing the fleet. The next stage is, therefore, the appraisal of the leasing proposition.

96

TABLE 6.4, *Example 6.3. Appraisal of Replacement of Old Fleet of Vehicles*

1. *Net Cash Investment*

	£
Cost of new vehicles	10 000
Less Realizable value of old vehicles	1 000
Total	9 000

2. *Annual and Residual Cash Flows*

Year	Cost savings	Tax on savings at 50%	Capital* allow- ances	Tax saved	Cash flow	PV factors for 8%	Present value
	£	£	£	£	£		£
1	2 500	—	6 000	3 000	5 500	0·926	5 093
2	2 500	1 250	1 000	500	1 750	0·857	1 501
3	2 500	1 250	750	375	1 625	0·794	1 290
4	—	1 250	—	—	(1 250)	0·735	(918)
	7 500	3 750	7 750	3 875	7 625		6 966
Residual value £4 000							
Less drawback of capital allowances			(1 750)	(875)	3 125	0·735	2 297
			6 000	3 000	10 750		9 263

* 60 per cent first year allowance, then 25 per cent writing down allowance.

LEASING DECISION

There are two considerations to be taken into account before appraising the leasing proposition. First, the net cash investment in respect of the leasing decision will be the net cash outlay on the new fleet, excluding the residual value of the old fleet.

Second, the net cost to the company is not the lease payments only. In the example, the leasing company is itself meeting some of the costs of running the vehicles and we shall be concerned only with the net cost to MO Transport. This net cost can be calculated as follows:

	£
Rental	620 per truck
Less	
Saving on road fund licence	50 per truck
Saving on maintenance	180 per truck
Net cost	390 per truck

We can now proceed to the evaluation of the leasing decision on the basis of the data shown in Table 6.5.

TABLE 6.5, *Example 6.3. Appraisal of Leasing New Fleet of Vehicles*

1. *Net Cash Investment*
   Cost of new vehicles £10 000

2. *Annual and Residual Cash Flows*

Year	Net Cost of leasing saved	Tax on saving at 50%	Capital allow- ances	Tax saved by capital allowances	Cash flow	PV factors for 8%	Present value
	£	£	£	£	£		£
1	3 900	—	6 000	3 000	6 900	0·926	6 389
2	3 900	1 950	1 000	500	2 450	0·857	2 100
3	3 900	1 950	750	375	2 325	0·794	1 846
4	—	1 950	—	—	(1 950)	0·735	(1 433)
	11 700	5 850	7 750	3 875	9 725		8 902
Residual value £4 000 *Less:* drawback of capital allowances			(1 750)	(875)	3 125	0·735	2 297
			6 000	3 000	12 850		11 199

In Example 6.3, the present value of the cash flows resulting from the purchase of the vehicles would be greater than the net cash investment. The return therefore is greater than the criterion rate. The profitability index for the leasing decision is 11 199/10 000 = 1·119.

The final decision in this case would depend upon the returns that could be earned on the investment of funds in other areas of the business (if any).

7 Financing Problems

The type of problems so far dealt with in our examination of the use of DCF have been concerned with circumstances where profitability has been used as the criterion to select, from among a range of investment projects, those that are most profitable. In other words, we have been dealing basic-ally with the *use* of funds within the business. The technique of DCF may, however, also be used when the capital structure of the business is con-sidered, and similar financial problems. Management is not only charged with the responsibility of ensuring that the return earned by the funds em-ployed within the business is maintained at as high a level as possible, but also of combining the various sources of funds employed, both borrowed and owner's, in such a way that the maximum return can be earned for the owners of the business, i.e., in the case of corporations, the equity share-holders.

Management will be comparing the relative costs of all the different types of funds employed in the business, or available to it, with the level of earn-ings on the capital employed, with a view to arriving at the best combina-tion of those funds from the point of view of the equity shareholder. This optimum position will be arrived at after considering the gearing that can be used in the capital structure of the business, the risk involved in incur-ring contractual obligations through borrowing, and any possible dilution effects on the holdings of existing shareholders.

Within this overall strategy of arranging the sources of funds it will be desirable to evaluate the relative merits of different forms of finance. This involves comparing the varying streams of cash flows associated with each source of finance. Some problems may also involve outlays of cash necessary to change from one source of finance to another in order to achieve net cost savings in financing the business.

When the relative values of streams of cash outlays and cost savings are being considered DCF will have an obvious part to play, but factors outside the realm of DCF will also exert a considerable effect, and, in many cases they may be of overriding importance in handling a particular problem.

SOURCES OF FUNDS FOR THE BUSINESS

Originally, the purpose in having a number of different sources of capital

99

to finance a business, was to appeal to as wide a range of investors as possible by dividing the capital into a number of different classes, each with different income and risk characteristics that would attract both the speculative and the conservative investor. Today, the reasoning behind the capital structure of a company is to achieve an optimum combination of sources of funds that will maximize the long-term value of the equity holders' funds.

The different classes of funds used include:

Ordinary Shares

Ordinary shares are those that, in general, bear the ultimate risks inherent in business operations, and that are entitled to the residual profits of the business after all other claims have been met. Within this class of shares also lies the voting control of the business, although the ordinary shares, as a whole, may be divided into voting and non-voting shares.

Ordinary shareholders are members of the company, and in consequence dividends cannot be paid on their shares unless there are earned profits from which payment can be made, and the payment is recommended by the directors.

Preference Shares

Usually this class of share is entitled to a fixed rate of dividend only, which must be paid before any payment can be made to ordinary shareholders. This dividend may be cumulative or non-cumulative. Usually, preference shareholders are also entitled to the repayment of their capital—sometimes with an element of premium—before any repayment can be made to ordinary shareholders. The shares do not normally carry the right to vote at meetings, although they may in certain circumstances, such as when the dividend is in arrears. Like ordinary shareholders, preference shareholders are members of the company, and the same restrictions on the payment of dividends apply to them.

Borrowed Funds

In complete contrast to the funds provided by the preference and ordinary shareholders, borrowed funds are derived from persons who are merely creditors of the company and who are not members, as are shareholders. As creditors, they may be secured or unsecured. In the USA the term 'Other People's Money' (OPM) is often used for this source of funds and serves to emphasize the distinction between borrowed funds, and owners' funds. Typical methods of borrowing funds are by means of debentures and secured or unsecured loans. Interest on debentures and loans is a charge against the profits of the business and, therefore, reduces the taxable profits.

No decision relating to the financing of a business should be made without fully taking into account the following factors:

1. The effect the decision will have on the risk factors in the business.
2. The way in which the gearing factor will be changed, and its effect on the equity holders.
3. Any possible dilution in the existing shareholders' interest in the capital and income of the business.
4. Its effect on the company from the point of view of flexibility in future financing operations.

The Risk Factor

A decision to add to the funds borrowed by the business will increase the risk element in the overall financing plan. Unlike shareholders, people who lend money to the business have a contractual right to the payment of interest and to the repayment, on the due date, of the amount lent. It is not in any way related to the *ability* of the business to pay. The risk to the business is that it may run into a period of recession and be unable to meet these commitments and so be put into liquidation. Any additional amount borrowed will increase this possibility and, consequently, increase the risk.

Gearing

The increase in the risk factor for the business also increases the risk attaching to the ordinary shares, holders of which are the ultimate risk bearers. Their compensation for this increase in risk is the effect the borrowed funds may have on the return that can be earned on their own funds, and is called *gearing** (or *leverage* in the United States). The advantage of gearing is that, if the business can earn on its employed capital more than it must pay for using borrowed funds, the difference between the two accrues to the benefit of the ordinary shareholders, and so increases their return. The effect that gearing can have on the return on equity funds can be quite significant.

Dilution

Public quoted companies in the United Kingdom are normally obliged to offer new ordinary shares to existing shareholders in proportion to their holdings whenever they wish to raise new funds by means of a share issue. This maintains the relative holdings of the shareholders one to another. Sometimes, however, as when there is a takeover bid or when the business enters into association with another company, this is not so, and consideration must be given to the effect such amalgamations may have in diluting

* For a fuller treatment of gearing see page 134.

the interests of the existing shareholders and the possible changes in the control of the company that may result. There is the apochryphal case of the company in Ireland which, on making a takeover bid for another company, lost sight of this fact, the shareholders in the company taken over finishing up with a majority of the shares in the company that had made the bid.

Flexibility

A decision to borrow £x million for a particular purpose at a particular time, cannot be made without considering the effect it will have on the business's borrowing powers in the future. There are limits to the borrowing capacity of a business, since the raising of every additional loan adds to the risks involved, both for the company and the lender.

A decision to substitute one form of borrowing for another at a lower rate of interest may increase the future debt capacity of the business, since the cost of servicing the existing borrowing has been reduced and will, therefore, absorb a lower proportion of the funds available to service debt.

The foregoing considerations are of such importance in any proposal relating to the provision of funds to the business that they may considerably constrain the part that DCF can play in such decisions, many of which, nevertheless, need to take into account the relative values of cash flows over varying periods of time. The DCF technique can therefore play a useful, if not perhaps predominant, role in evaluating these factors so that a rational judgement can be exercised when these are under discussion.

Refunding Operations

Management should continually monitor the various sources of funds employed to ensure that their cost is kept to a minimum. Such differences can arise because:

1. Interest rates and preference dividend yields alter making that source more or less costly compared with the cost of existing funds.
2. Changes take places in the tax structure of the country within which the company operates which change the relative net of tax cost of different sources.

Interest rates may vary considerably at different stages in the economic cycle. Where a company is borrowing money over a 20 to 25 year period the nominal interest rate may differ markedly from the current market rates during the currency of that loan. For example, in the UK in 1972, there were in existence many debenture stocks carrying interest rates of 3 to 6 per cent, e.g., Unilever $3\frac{3}{4}$ per cent, Cable & Wireless 5 per cent, whereas the market rate for new loans was over 10 per cent at one time.

Unless there are obstacles to repayment, there are good arguments for refunding high-cost borrowing in periods of low interest rates. A saving of 1 per cent after tax is significant when compared with the difficulty of improving the return on capital employed by a similar amount.

TAXATION

The way that tax structure changes affect the relative cost of different sources of funds is illustrated by the changes that have taken place in the UK since 1965. During the whole of this period, *interest* has been a charge against profit before tax and therefore has attracted tax relief. Before 1965, the relief was at the rate of $56\frac{1}{4}$ per cent; between 1965 and 1973 it ranged from 40 to 45 per cent; from 1973 it is at 50 per cent. Thus, an 8 per cent loan currently costs 4 per cent after tax.

Dividends on the other hand are paid out of after tax profits. The effect on these of the UK tax changes is shown in Table 7.1. Before 1965 the tax paid by a company was, as far as the income tax element was concerned, a prepayment of the tax on the shareholders of their share of the corporate profits. When a dividend was declared, the additional cost of the payment was the net cost of the dividend only. The only difference was the effect of profits tax which was borne by the company.

Between 1965 and 1973, the tax on dividends was a second tier tax on corporate earnings and the cost of the dividend became the *gross* amount.

TABLE 7.1. *Effect of UK Tax Changes*

	Pre 1965		*1965–1973*			*1973 onwards*	
		£			£		£
Taxable Profit		100			100		100
Profits tax 15%			Corporation			Corporation	
Income Tax 41·25%	56		Tax 40%		40	Tax 50%	50
		44			60		50
Dividends							
Gross	50		Gross	50		Gross	50
			Less			*Less*†	
Less tax at			tax	21		Act	15
standard rate	21	29			29		35
			*Schedule F Tax		21		
Retained profit		15			10		15

* Tax deducted at source and paid over to the revenue.

† The dividend would be declared as a net £35 and the tax imputed to that dividend would be paid over to the revenue in the form of Advanced Corporation Tax. The shareholder then computes the gross value of the dividend to him by multiplying the net amount he receives by 10/7 ($35 \times 10/7 = 50$)

This changed the relative cost of preference dividends (gross out of after tax earnings) and interest which continued to attract tax relief.

From 1973 onwards the UK reverted to a system similar to that prevailing before 1965 modelled on the French imputation system. Although corporation tax remains, the shareholder is paid a net dividend. A portion of the corporation tax paid by the company (currently three-fifths) is imputed to his dividend. In the example, the dividend from the shareholder's point of view is £50 less 30 per cent tax = £35. The imputed tax must be paid over by the company to the revenue as an advance payment of its final corporation tax liability (Advanced Corporation Tax).

It can be seen that the relative cost of interest and dividends net of tax under the present system varies only by the difference between the rate at which tax is imputed to dividends and the corporation tax rate (at the time of writing 30 per cent and 50 per cent respectively except for small companies where the rate is 40 per cent). Thus, an 8 per cent preference dividend has a net of tax cost of 5·6 per cent, whereas an 8 per cent debenture carries a net cost of 4 per cent.

This differential between the net cost of interest and dividends is still sufficiently large to warrant close attention by management to the possibilities of altering the fundamental balance between shareholders' funds and borrowed funds. In particular, if it is possible to replace a 7 per cent preference share by a 7 per cent debenture, or one carrying a marginally higher rate of interest, for example, the return on the ordinary shareholders' funds may be improved.

Since both preference and ordinary dividends are subject to the same rules, the above remarks relating to the cost of preference dividends apply equally to the cost of ordinary dividends. In Britain, where the reduction of capital requires the sanction of the court, the possibilities of replacing ordinary shares with borrowed funds are limited. It is instructive, however, to see the effect of the corporation tax system in the United States, where it has been in existence for many years. There, a corporation has the power to purchase its own shares, thus directly reducing the issued capital. The combination of a corporation tax system and the ability to reduce the issued capital easily has brought about major changes in the balance between borrowed and shareholders' funds.

Because the legal requirements in the United Kingdom are different, however, it is unlikely that these fundamental relationships will be radically changed in a short space of time, but there will be a continuing trend on the American pattern. This is evidenced by the large volume of debentures that have been on offer since 1965, and the relative dearth of new equity issues.

USE OF DCF IN REFUNDING OPERATIONS

Refunding is the term used when a business retires one issue in its capital structure and replaces it with another issue, which frequently happens when the life of one form of borrowing is drawing to an end and a new source of funds, to replace the one that is to be lost, must be found.

This section of the book, however, is concerned with a more restricted area of refunding operations: when management is actively considering the retirement of one source of funds, not because its life is drawing to an end, but because it is concerned with the cost differential of the existing funds as compared with new funds it might use.

The refunding operation will involve the outlay of part of the firm's cash resources on expenses connected with the retirement of the old issue and the marketing of the new one. Such expenses would include:

1. Any premium payable on the old issue due to its early retirement.
2. Expenses of retiring the old issue.
3. Expenses of the new issue, e.g., postage, printing, underwriting commission, issuing house fees, etc.
4. Double interest if the two issues overlap, or any *additional* costs of bridging finance to cover a period between the redemption of the old issue and the inflow of funds from the new issue.

This outlay of funds will be in competition with the demands for funds for investment in other uses within the business, in the same way as any other investment project. The investment of £x of the available funds for a refunding operation means that they will not be available for employment elsewhere, and for this reason it must be ascertained whether or not the net savings that can be achieved by this investment of funds represents an adequate return on the net cash investment as compared with other alternative forms of investment available to the business.

Suitability of DCF in the Refunding Decision

It is sometimes questioned whether DCF is suitable for any stage in the appraisal of a refunding operation if other factors that must be taken into account are of such importance, and in particular whether the investment of funds in a refunding operation does compete with other projects for the funds available. The argument here is that the refunding operation may itself actually enlarge the available volume of funds.

When the business replaces one loan with a new loan at a lower rate of interest, the burden of borrowing on the business is reduced and leaves a larger margin of unused debt capacity, which makes the borrowing of further funds easier. This would not be true if preference shares are replaced by new borrowing since this may further restrict the borrowing capacity of the business, as the assets available for security of borrowing are now absorbed, at least in part, by existing financing. Both these types of refunding operation may, by their effect on the return on equity funds, improve the possibility of raising new shareholders' funds in the future.

It is submitted, however, that DCF has a role to play in this decision.

105

Quite irrespective of the effect the decision may have on the ability of the business to raise additional funds in the future, refunding will absorb some of the capital employed in the business, and if the profitability of the business is to be maintained such a use of funds should, among other things, be subject to the same tests of profitability as any other project. Certainly the rate of return, as shown by the DCF computation, will not necessarily be the deciding factor, but the rate of return that can be earned by employing the funds in this particular way should be taken into account when the decision is made.

Before examining the way in which the data should be handled in making the DCF appraisal, it should be pointed out that there is relatively little risk attached to this decision. The future savings can be accurately calculated as they are the difference between two contractual rates of interest or dividend, and the cost factors in the net cash investment should be capable of close estimation.

NET CASH INVESTMENT

The net cash investment in the refunding operation consists of the various expenses noted on page 105. In addition to the outlays themselves their tax consequences must be considered. In general, the expenses connected with a new issue and any premium payable on the redemption of an old one will not be deductible for tax purposes, and the before tax and after tax costs will be the same. Additional interest costs in the changeover period will be allowable for tax purposes and, when taken into account, must be adjusted to the after tax figure.

ANNUAL SAVINGS

The return resulting from the net cash investment is the saving in cost as between the interest or fixed dividend payable on the old issue, and that payable on the new issue. As interest is a charge allowable for tax purposes, the interest in these calculations should be the after tax cost.

TIME HORIZON

Normally the length of time an existing issue has still to run will be less than the life that will be set for a new issue. If, for example, it is proposed to replace by a new loan one that still has ten years to run, it is likely that the life set for the new loan will be twenty to twenty-five years. This provides no basis for comparison beyond the remaining life of the existing loan, and as residual values are not appropriate in this type of problem the life of the project for DCF purposes would be 10 years.

Example 7.1

Peraco Ltd has outstanding an 8 per cent unsecured loan of £1 500 000 that has a further twelve years to run before it must be repaid. The company has the option of repaying the loan at any time before maturity at a premium of 3 per cent. Since the issue was made, interest rates have fallen considerably, and the company is now considering the issue of £1 500 000 5 per cent debentures with a a life of 25 years to replace the unsecured loan.

It is anticipated that the costs connected with the new issue would amount to £35 000, and that the new issue would be made two months before the repayment of the old one. The company could earn 3 per cent on the short-term placing of its surplus cash resources.

The tax rate is 50 per cent, and the company has other projects available on which it can earn 10 per cent after tax.

The problem should be broken down into the two major elements of net cash investment and annual cash flows, as before (residual value is not applicable). As the annual saving is a constant amount, the gross saving and the related tax can be evaluated by using the table in Appendix B. The computations relating to the problem are shown in Table 7.2. It can be

TABLE 7.2, *Example 7.1. Evaluation of Exchanging one form of Borrowing for another*

		£
1. *Net Cash Investment*		
Expenses of new issue		35 000
Premium on redemption of old issue		
£1 500 000 × 3/100		45 000
Net interest cost for two months		
5−3% of £1 500 000 × 2/12	£5 000	
Less tax at 50%	2 500	
		2 500
Total net cash investment		82 500
2. *Annual Cash Flows*		
Annual interest saving 8% less 5% on		
£1 500 000=£45 000 p.a.		
Tax on saving at 50%=£22 500 p.a.		
Present values at 10% discount rate		£
Interest saving £45 000 p.a. receivable		
annually for twelve years 45 000 × 6·814		306 630
Tax on saving £22 500 p.a. payable annually for		
years 2 to 13 (i.e., one year in arrear of savings)		
22 500 × (7·103 − 0·909)		139 365
Net present value		167 265

seen there that the use of funds on this project would produce a return well in excess of the 10 per cent that can be earned on other projects and gives a profitability index of 167 265/82 500 = 2·027.

Example 7.2
The board of directors of Stampo Ltd have recently considered the position of the preference shares issued by their company. The nominal value of

the shares amounts to £500 000 bearing a cumulative dividend of 7 per cent. It would be possible to redeem the shares by offering 110p for each £1 share. The directors estimate that they could issue an unsecured loan of £500 000 repayable in 20 years' time carrying an interest rate of 6 per cent. The directors plan to redeem the preference issue on 1 March and to make the unsecured loan issue on 1 May. Bridging finance would be available at 6 per cent. The cost of the operation would be £12 000.

The company's criterion rate of return is 8 per cent after tax, and the current tax rate is 50 per cent.

The calculations relating to Example 7.2 are shown in Table 7.3 from which it can be seen that the sum of the present values amounts to £82 366, compared with the net cash investment of £60 417, giving a profitability index of 1·36. It will be seen that in this example the time horizon for the project has been taken at 20 years, which is the life of the new unsecured loan stock. This is because there is no obligation on the company to redeem the preference shares and there is, therefore, a comparable figure on which to evaluate the savings in each of the years.

TABLE 7.3, *Example 7.2. Evaluation of Replacement of Preference Shares by Borrowing*

		£	£
1. *Net Cash Investment*			
Premium on redemption of preference shares			50 000
Expenses of redemption and new issue			12 000
Interest saving on bridging finance			
Cost of preference dividend for two months		5 833	
Less Advance corporation tax		1 750	
		4 083	
Interest on bridging finance for two months			
at 6%	5 000		
Less tax at 50%	2 500		
		2 500	
			(1 583)
Total Net Cash Investment			60 417
2. *Annual Cash Flows*			
Annual Saving (net):			
Cost of 7% dividend 7% *less* 30% ACT=4·9%			24 500
6% loan interest gross		30 000	
Less tax relief		15 000	
			15 000
			9 500

Present Values:

Net dividend saved: £24 500 p.a. years 1–20 24 500 × 9·818	240 541
Cost of interest gross years 1–20 30 000 × 9·818	(294 540)
Corporation tax saved on interest payment years 2–21	
15 000 × (10·017 − 0·926)	136 365
	82 366

Evaluating Alternative Issues

In problems concerned with raising additional finance, management's task is to select the method of financing that shows the best return for the business. As with many other DCF problems, management should be critical of all proposals submitted to ensure that all alternative methods of achieving the financing operation are fully explored.

Each alternative method of financing will involve differing streams of payments in the future, such streams of payments being made up of interest, dividends, or repayment of principal. DCF can be of considerable assistance in selecting the proposal in which the cost has the lowest present value, and which is, therefore, the one that will produce maximum values for the shareholders in the future. (This will be understood if it is realized that the profit potential of the business consists of a series of future receipts with a given present value. The payments in respect of the proposed finance will reduce this future stream of receipts, and the smaller their present value the greater will be the present value remaining for the shareholders.)

In this use of DCF, the cash flows resulting from an investment are no longer being compared with the cash outlay on that investment. The problem is solely concerned with the present value of future streams of payments. The differences that are being compared are the timing of the future payments, differences in the cost of interest, etc., and the pattern of repayments of the principal sum.

Example 7.3

Copond Ltd is going through a period of rapid expansion and the board are actively considering raising additional funds to finance their future expansion. The firm needs a further £400 000 to carry it over the next few years, and the board have been presented with two proposals for raising the funds required.

Proposal A is to raise an unsecured loan of £400 000 carrying an interest rate of 6 per cent, for a period of 20 years. The whole of the £400 000 is to be repaid at the end of the twentieth year.

Proposal B is to issue £400 000 $5\frac{1}{2}$ per cent debentures with a life of twenty-five years. No repayments of the principal are to be made for the first five years, but thereafter £20 000 of the debentures must be redeemed at the end of each year.

The current tax rate is 40 per cent and the company can earn 8 per cent on the funds employed in the business.

The procedure for dealing with this type of problem is, first, to calculate the net cash outgoings in respect of each alternative for each year of its life. The present value of the cash flows is then calculated and the alternatives compared. This process is shown in Tables 7.4 and 7.5, from which it can be seen that the net present value of the stream of payments that

109

would result from the implementation of Proposal A is less than the stream of payments for Proposal B and, therefore, Proposal A would be more advantageous for the business.

TABLE 7.4, *Example 7.3. Present Value of Payments for Unsecured Loan Alternative*

	£
Annual interest cost 6% of £400 000	
Less tax at 40%	14 400
Terminal payment	400 000
Present value of cash flows	
£14 400 payable annually for 25 years at 8% 14 400 × 10·675	153 720
£400 000 payable at the end of 25 years 400 000 × 0·146	58 400
Total present value of cash flows	212 120

TABLE 7.5, *Example 7.3. Present Value of Payments for the Debenture Alternative*

Year	Interest after tax	Repayment of principal	Total payments	PV factor for 8%	Present value
	£	£	£		£
1	13 200	—	13 200	0·926	12 223
2	13 200	—	13 200	0·857	11 312
3	13 200	—	13 200	0·794	10 481
4	13 200	—	13 200	0·735	9 702
5	13 200	—	13 200	0·681	8 989
6	13 200	20 000	33 200	0·630	20 916
7	12 540	20 000	32 540	0·583	18 971
8	11 880	20 000	31 880	0·540	17 215
9	11 220	20 000	31 220	0·500	15 610
10	10 560	20 000	30 560	0·463	14 149
11	9 900	20 000	29 900	0·429	12 827
12	9 240	20 000	29 240	0·397	11 608
13	8 580	20 000	28 580	0·368	10 517
14	7 920	20 000	27 920	0·340	9 493
15	7 260	20 000	27 260	0·315	8 587
16	6 600	20 000	26 600	0·292	7 767
17	5 940	20 000	25 940	0·270	7 004
18	5 280	20 000	25 280	0·250	6 320
19	4 620	20 000	24 620	0·232	5 712
20	3 960	20 000	23 960	0·215	5 151
21	3 300	20 000	23 300	0·199	4 637
22	2 640	20 000	22 640	0·184	4 166
23	1 980	20 000	21 980	0·170	3 737
24	1 320	20 000	21 320	0·158	3 369
25	660	20 000	20 660	0·146	3 016
Total present value of cash flows					243 479

The sum of the actual payments in respect of A are, in fact, higher than the actual payments in respect of B, since the whole of the principal is outstanding for the entire period. If the rate of discounting being used is directly

110

related to the return that can be earned by the employment of funds within the business, the 'stretching' of the repayments right up to the end of the loan period more than compensates for the extra costs involved.

In common with other financing problems there will be a number of other factors to take into account. In the case under review, the two principal ones that would need to be considered are:

1. The debenture proposal would involve security being given over the assets of the business, and this might reduce the ability of the business to raise additional borrowed funds in the future.
2. Proposal B provides for earlier repayment of the principal sum, therefore, the debt ratio of the company will fall steadily after the fifth year, quite apart from the normal fall due to retentions. This may enable additional funds to be borrowed in the later years when the ratio has been substantially reduced.

DCF and Investment in Shares

One area where there has been little application of DCF is in the field of investment in quoted shares. The point is illustrated here because it will have some relevance to the methods of determining the cost of capital treated in chapter 9. The attitudes of the investing public will be of importance in that context, particularly the way in which they regard the return appropriate to individual shares.

An investment of funds in shares is usually made with two purposes in mind: to provide an annual return in the form of the dividend receivable on the shares held; and to secure capital appreciation in the value of the shares when they are sold. These two factors make up the overall return on an investment. When comparing alternative investments, both these factors are considered and the shares showing the highest combined return selected.

The pattern of cash flows for a share investment is similar to that for an investment in plant and machinery. There is an initial outlay of funds when the investment is made and this is followed by a series of annual cash flows and a residual value. In this case, the net cash investment will be made up of the cost of the shares plus the attendant expenses. The expenses will not be an allowable charge for tax purposes when the purchaser is an investment company, but will be allowed in the case of a dealing company.

The income the shares will earn will consist of the dividend receivable, which is net of imputed tax. Individual investors may also be subject to a surcharge or able to claim refunds. Of much more importance when deciding to invest in shares is the residual value, in this case the proceeds from the sale of the shares (less expenses of sale). If, when sold, the amount realized is greater than the cost of the shares then there will be a capital gains tax liability on the difference. A loss on sale will qualify for relief against other capital gains and the tax on the loss may be recouped. These rules will be modified in respect of shares purchased before 5 April 1965.

The calculation of the after tax return that would be earned on an investment then proceeds along the same lines as a normal DCF calculation.

Example 7.4

Mr AB is considering the purchase of 200 ordinary shares in company X. The market value of the shares to buy is 250p and the expenses of the purchase would be £12. The shares are to be purchased as an investment, and Mr AB's evaluation of them is based upon an assumption that the current dividend (net) of 11·75p per share will increase to 13·2p in the third year after the purchase, and to 14·7p in the fourth year. He would expect to sell the holding at the end of the fourth year at a price of 350p incurring selling costs of £9. Assume that the effective rate of capital gains tax is 20 per cent.

The method of calculating the rate of return on this investment is shown in Table 7.6. The use of DCF in appraising the relative merits of various shares

TABLE 7.6. *Use of the DCF Method in Investment in Ordinary Shares*

1. *Net Cash Investment*

	£
Purchase price of shares	500
Plus expenses of purchase	12
Total cost	512

2. *Annual and Residual Cash flows*

Year	Net dividends	PV factors for 11%	Present value	PV factors for 12%	Present value
	£		£		£
1	23·5	0·901	21·17	0·893	20·99
2	23·5	0·812	19·08	0·797	18·73
3	26·4	0·731	19·30	0·712	18·80
4	29·4	0·659	19·37	0·636	18·70
	102·8		78·92		77·22
*Residual Value**					
	655	0·659	431·64	0·636	416·58
	757·8		510·56		493·80

* Residual value is calculated as follows:

	£
Sale value of shares	700
Less expenses of sale	9
	691
Less capital gains tax at 20% on £691, less net cost of £512	36
	655

requires a great deal of discipline in evaluating the factors that must be taken into account. It is no longer possible to say 'I will buy this share as I expect the dividend will rise and there will be a rise in the price of the share'. Explicit values must be placed on both these factors. In using the DCF method, *all* the factors must be given definite values. This discipline is, in itself, a good thing, for if that method is used, greater care must be taken in evaluating the data upon which the investment decision is based and, inevitably, will result in a more rational decision. As in other problems, the investor will select investments by ranking alternatives in order of profitability.

Turning to the costs of capital to a business, it will be seen that the cost of the ordinary shareholders' funds will be based largely on the long-term return investors expect from purchasing the company's shares. This will be compared with returns from other companies and other forms of investment, and there will be some movement to a common yardstick of return.

8 Uncertainty and Risk

CRITICAL NATURE OF INVESTMENT DECISIONS

Decisions relating to capital investment are among the most difficult, and at the same time the most critical, management has to make. Critical, because the effects of such decisions will have far reaching influences on the business's profitability for many years into the future. Once the investment decision has been made, the ill effects which may result from that decision cannot be corrected by what might otherwise be good management—they can only be mitigated. If, for example, an oil refinery is located where inland communications are difficult, and where modern supertankers cannot berth, the ill effects of that decision will depress the profitability of the business until the refinery can be replaced. The decision has affected the underlying structure of the business and the base on which it operates.

Such decisions are difficult because of the many uncertainties in forecasting future trends. In planning future operations in a modern industrial society, the rate of technological, economic, and social change is so rapid that forecasting the future environment in which the business will be operating can be a hazardous process. Moreover, the tempo of such changes is not lessening, but rather increasing, in intensity.

INFLUENCE OF GOVERNMENT ON UNCERTAINTY

Business decisions are primarily a balancing of prospective rewards against risks, as far as can be foreseen. Any increase in the risk factor through the widening of the area of uncertainty may lead to opportunities for beneficial investments being missed, simply because the uncertainties are so great and the range of possible variations in the uncertain factors unknown.

This, perhaps, should be more widely recognized by governments. The business community can make decisions on future policies only in the light of the economic and social environment in which they operate. The more government action infiltrates into the structure of this environment, and the more government policy in its various spheres (but in particular its policy relating to the national economy) is subject to sudden changes in emphasis and direction, the greater the uncertainty management faces when planning investments.

The various economic crises in most countries, and in the United Kingdom in particular, have resulted in massive changes in economic and fiscal policy. If governments wish businesses to operate with maximum efficiency, and to make rational decisions affecting the future of their operations by using modern techniques to quantify the various factors involved in reaching that decision, then governments should create an environment in which uncertainty is reduced to a minimum.

Unless steps are taken along these lines, there are prospects that uncertainty alone may defeat economic growth. Competitive forces and technological change themselves present considerable uncertainty in any business decision. These are unavoidable, but efforts should be made to reduce avoidable uncertainty where it is at all possible.

DANGERS IN AVOIDING RISK

It may be thought that by avoiding risks, i.e., by deciding not to proceed with projects that contain a large element of uncertainty, management can shield the business from the risk element. Further thought will show that this will not necessarily be so. Typically, the riskiest investment proposals are those concerned with launching new products, and research and development expenditure, but these activities are essential investments if a business is to survive and to grow. Any business that does not generate new ideas and products is likely to be overtaken by the competitive spirit of its rivals.

If the management of a business is overawed by the uncertainties of proposals that are put forward, or becomes unwilling to take the risks inherent in making decisions, the business will become stagnant. In other words, failure to invest in such projects exposes the business to a much greater potential risk, that of competitors overtaking it in technical and marketing know-how and leaving it to become old-fashioned and uncompetitive.

ROLE OF DCF IN HANDLING RISK AND UNCERTAINTY

Where there is an element of uncertainty, management, in appraising an investment, will have less difficulty in coming to a decision if it can obtain some idea of the magnitude of the uncertainty, for the extent of the uncertainty is commensurate with the extent of the risk. If there were no uncertainty there would be no risk other than that proceeding from a thoroughly bad decision.

Given that there will always be some uncertainty in investment decisions, it may yet be proved that the greatest contribution to investment appraisal made by the DCF technique is to provide a framework for measuring the degree of uncertainty, thereby reducing it to a quantifiable factor for making an investment decision.

The same techniques developed to deal with uncertainty can also be used to extend the depth of analysis employed in the appraisal system. The rate of return on an investment is extremely sensitive to changes in some of the elements used in its appraisal. If management is made aware of the effects on the rate of return of changes in these elements, the depth of the problem will at once be apparent, like adding a third dimension to a two-dimensional drawing, and simplify the decision-making process. These are significant contributions to management techniques that have yet to become widely appreciated.

DCF relies on forecasting techniques, since it is based upon estimates of all the factors that enter into the calculations. As it is primarily concerned with investment in fixed assets, it deals with forecasts for a number of years ahead. This forward forecasting will cover a wide range of values, many of which may be outside the control of management, or influenced by factors outside their control, i.e., the state of the economy, and the level and incidence of taxation.

One of the disciplines DCF introduces into the firm's forecasting is the obligation to put a value on *all* the factors that must be taken into account, irrespective of whether or not there are uncertainties. This means that, instead of dismissing any factor as being incapable of evaluation, some effort must be made to put a value on it. This means that the factor will be given thought and consideration that otherwise it might not receive. This may present problems to the forecasting team, but it is important that every factor should be subjected to analysis and appraisal.

When there are uncertainties in the data relating to a project possible ways of limiting them should be found first. If, for example, one of the uncertain factors is the cost behaviour in the business, studies may be carried out that will limit the unknowns. When all possibilities are exhausted, the limits of the uncertain elements that remain should be defined prior to inclusion in the DCF solution. Then, when the project is running, the areas of uncertainty already defined should be those subject to the maximum amount of control, particularly those to which the rate of return is more than usually sensitive. The way in which these factors are controlled will vitally affect the ultimate profitability of the project.

Finally, it must be remembered that the result of the DCF appraisal will be, at best, no better than the data that has been provided by the budgeting techniques used. If the business is to achieve a higher than average degree of success in picking out profitable projects for investment, its whole forecasting system must be of the highest standard. DCF will be of little help to management if it is used to appraise inaccurate data. 'Post-audit' techniques, reviewing investment projects at intervals after they have been approved, will prove worth while in ensuring a satisfactory standard of basic budgeting.

Probability

Some investment projects can be appraised more accurately than others.

116

For a project involving the replacement of plant and machinery, firm quotations for the items to be purchased may already have been received, and the potential savings in labour and other costs will be capable of fairly close evaluation. The only real uncertainties may lie in the life and residual value of the plant, and taxation and other changes resulting from, say, changes in government policy. On the other hand, projects that involve laying down new plant for manufacturing an additional product will introduce a number of uncertainties. Market research and the launching of the new product will require the investment of substantial funds. Sales volume, selling price, costs of both marketing and production, as well as other uncertainties will also be present, hence the DCF rate of return will vary in accordance with the accuracy of the forecasting of these factors.

Of principal importance to management will be the degree of certainty achieved in forecasting the rate of return. What is the probability that the rate of return will be 10 per cent and what are the probabilities of rates on either side of the value? The forecast rate of return is the bare bones of the solution. What management wants to do, is to clothe it with flesh that will give it contours, so that the examination of any DCF problem can be carried out in depth, which is not possible when only a single rate solution is given.

If this type of analysis is possible when comparing investment proposals, as a preliminary to ranking them in order of desirability, due attention can be given to the probability of the forecast returns being achieved, and the prospect of returns being higher or lower than that forecast. A project, in which there is a strong possibility that the forecast rate will be exceeded, is clearly a better prospect than one with an equivalent forecast rate but where there is a strong possibility of its not being reached.

Moreover, when a project is in the planning and appraisal stage and not yet a firm commitment, management may well be interested in the effect on the rate of return of varying the value of one of the factors. For example, if the price range of the product is changed, what effect will this have on the rate of return? The use of the techniques developed for risk analysis enables an assessment to be made of changes in the value of any of the factors that have been incorporated in the solution, and so furnishes management with a further analytical tool to assist in decision-making.

Use of the Computer
A sophisticated system for analysing risk and uncertainty, and to measure the effect of changes in any of the component factors, will usually require the use of a computer. This book will not attempt to go into the detailed aspects of the computer programming involved in using the technique, since problems that arise are not difficult for a competent programmer to solve, and the mathematical basis employed is a recognized technique in the field

of operational research. Standard package programs are already available for those who wish to use the technique in their appraisal system.

For the business that does not own or rent a computer, facilities are available at various centres for programming special problems or for supplying standard programs and renting machine time. The use of this technique therefore need not be restricted to large firms with internal computer experience.

In this chapter, attention will be concentrated on the overall management approach to risk analysis, the factors involved, and the way in which a solution to the problem should be approached.

Estimating the Range of Rates of Return Without a Computer

When, for any reason, it is impossible, or impracticable, to use a computer for this type of problem, a manual method that will give a fair approximation of the spread of possible rates of return can be employed. In the DCF calculations used so far in this book, we have used data based on the assumption that it is possible to give a single value to each of the factors under consideration, e.g., 'The project has a life of eight years', 'The rate of tax is 40 per cent', 'The increase in annual revenue will be £5000', and so on. In practice, of course, these are the figures or values that we consider are most likely to emerge, and, in the event, these values may prove to be greater or less than those actually achieved.

ESTABLISHING THE RANGE OF DATA

The first step in approaching risk analysis is to start asking questions about the possible limits in both directions for all the values that are to be used. If the increase in revenue involved in the DCF calculation is £5000, we may find, with reasonable certainty, that the increase in revenue will not exceed £6000 nor be less than £4000, and that £5000 is the most likely figure that will be achieved.

This process will be repeated for all the factors that are to be used, so that for each of them we have a value for the possible upper and lower limits of likely variations in the values contained in the calculations. As a result of this process there will be available for all, or some, of the factors involved, three values:

1. The 'possible best' value.
2. The 'most probable' value.
3. The 'possible worst' value.

By taking all the 'possible best' values for all the factors, we can use these to calculate a 'possible best' rate of return; by taking all the 'most probable' factors we can calculate the 'most probable' rate of return; and by taking all the 'possible worst' factors we can calculate the 'possible worst' rate of return.

118

This method, although it will not enable management to calculate the degree of probability that any particular rate of return will be achieved will at least show the theoretical limits to the variations of the rate of return from that forecast.

Example 8.1

An investment project involves an estimated outlay of £20 000, and the limits to the outlay are believed to be £19 000 and £22 000. The increase in revenue, before depreciation, that is expected from the project will vary from £5200 to £6000 with the most probable value being £5500. Depending on the impact of technological change, the project will have an estimated useful life of between four and seven years, the most likely duration being five years. At the end of the fourth year, the residual value of the plant is expected to be £1200, after the fifth year £400, and after the seventh year £100. No change can be foreseen in the rate of taxation (50 per cent) and capital allowances. Tax advisers state that it would be advisable to take advantage of the 100 per cent first year capital allowances.

What is the most likely rate of return, and the upper and lower limits to the rate of return based upon the estimates made?

Table 8.1 gives the data for calculating the probable rate of return, and combines all the most probable values of the factors in the calculation, from which it can be seen that the most probable rate of return is 12 per cent.

TABLE 8.1, *Example 8.1. Calculation of the Most Probable Rate of Return*

1. *Net Cash Investment*

	£
Cost of plant, etc.	20 000

2. *Annual and Residual Cash Flows*

Year	Increase in revenue £	Tax at 50% £	Capital allowances £	Tax saved £	Cash flow £	PV factors for 12%	Present value £
1	5 500	—	20 000	10 000	15 500	0·893	13 841
2	5 500	2 750	—	—	2 750	0·797	2 192
3	5 500	2 750	—	—	2 750	0·712	1 958
4	5 500	2 750	—	—	2 750	0·636	1 746
5	5 500	2 750	—	—	2 750	0·567	1 560
6	—	2 750	—	—	(2 750)	0·507	(1 394)
	27 500	13 750	20 000	10 000	23 750		19 903

Residual value
Sale of plant £400
Less drawback of capital allowances

			(400)	(200)	200	0·507	101
			19 600	9 800	23 950		20 004

119

Table 8.2 gives the data for the possible worst values for all the factors, from which we can see that the possible worst rate of return is zero.

TABLE 8.2, *Example 8.1: Calculation of the Possible Worst Rate of Return*

1. *Net Cash Investment* £
   Cost of plant, etc. 22 000

2. *Annual and Residual Cash Flows*

Year	Increase in revenue	Tax at 50%	Capital allow-ances	Tax saved	Cash flow	PV factors	Present value
	£	£	£	£	£		£
1	5 200	—	22 000	11 000	16 200	Since the cash	
2	5 200	2 600	—	—	2 600	flows exactly equal	
3	5 200	2 600	—	—	2 600	the investment the	
4	5 200	2 600	—	—	2 600	rate of return	
5	—	2 600	—	—	(2 600)	is zero	
	20 800	10 400	22 000	11 000	21 400		

Residual Value
Sale of plant £1 200
Less drawback of capital

allowances			(1 200)	(600)	600		
			20 800	10 400	22 000		

Table 8.3 gives the data for the possible best values for all the factors, and shows a possible best rate of return of just under 25 per cent.

TABLE 8.3, *Example 8.1. Calculation of the Possible Best Rate of Return*

1. *Net Cash Investment* £
   Cost of plant, etc. 19 000

2. *Annual and Residual Cash Flows*

Year	Increase in revenue	Tax at 50%	Capital allow-ances	Tax saved	Cash flow	PV factors for 25%	Present value
	£	£	£	£	£		£
1	6 000	—	19 000	9 500	15 500	0·800	12 400
2	6 000	3 000	—	—	3 000	0·640	1 920
3	6 000	3 000	—	—	3 000	0·512	1 536
4	6 000	3 000	—	—	3 000	0·410	1 230
5	6 000	3 000	—	—	3 000	0·328	984
6	6 000	3 000	—	—	3 000	0·262	786
7	6 000	3 000	—	—	3 000	0·210	630
8	—	3 000	—	—	(3 000)	0·168	(504)
	42 000	21 000	19 000	9 500	30 500		18 982

Residual Value
Sale of plant £100
Less drawback of capital

allowances			(100)	(50)	50	0·168	8
			18 900	9 450	30 550		18 990

120

The rates of return calculated in the preceding three tables have set the upper and lower rates of return, as well as the most probable rate of return. It has thus gone one step further than the calculation of a single rate of return, and has provided management with an indication of the possible variations in the rate that may be earned on either side of the forecast rate. Some of the uncertainty inherent in the project has been removed, in so far as some definition has been given to the possible spread of the rate of return.

From the nature of probability theory, however, it is possible to give some indication of the probability of different intermediate rates of return being achieved. If the three rates of return for Example 8.1 are plotted on a graph, as in Fig. 8.1, the lowest rate of return at A, the most probable rate

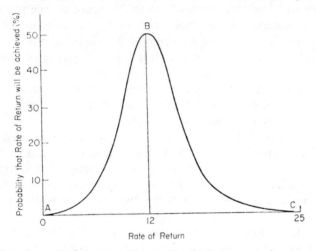

Figure 8.1. Example 8.1. Approximate distribution curve of rates of return

at B, and the highest rate at C, the three points can be connected with a curve of the general shape shown, which approximates to the general shape of a distribution curve. The approximate degree of probability of any particular rate being achieved can be read off from this graph.

Uncertainty and Risk—Using the Computer

The upper and lower rates of return calculated in Example 8.1 were based on the assumption that *all* the most favourable predictions or *all* the least favourable predictions will fall together. As a result, Fig. 8.1 gives only some indication of the degree of probability of achieving intermediate rates of return. A more subtle tool is needed if management is to be able to forecast with any degree of accuracy, the real distribution curve of possible rates of return for a project.

In real life it is most likely that there will be a combination of good and bad outcomes incorporated in the final result. The way in which such factors combine in any particular circumstance will depend upon the degree of probability that any given value for each factor will emerge. This degree of probability will, in turn, depend upon the distribution curve of probabilities for that factor. The rate of return that results from the random combination of factors is a reflection of those values. The advent of the computer, and the application of mathematical techniques to business problems now makes possible relatively simple solutions to such problems.

MONTE CARLO TECHNIQUE

The method of calculating the distribution curve of possible rates of return for any investment problem is derived from what is known as the *Monte Carlo technique*. The name comes from the games of chance played at the casino there. Roulette, for example, is a game that involves the random selection of numbers, since for each spin of the wheel, each of the numbers has an equal chance of coming up. Over a long sequence of games, each number should come up the same number of times.

When the possible chances of a value being chosen are not equal, then a series of random selections should reflect that fact. If, for example, a number of men from a certain population is selected at random and their heights are measured, most of the men would be found to be between, say, 5 ft 9 in and 6 ft. There would be very few men with a height of less than 5 ft or greater than 6 ft 6 in. In other words, if a sufficiently large sample of the population is selected on a random basis, a distribution curve of the heights of the group would accurately reflect the distribution of height of the male population.

To take into account uncertainty and risk in any investment problem, it is necessary to prepare, for each of the factors relevant to the problem, a distribution curve that shows the probability of any particular value being achieved for that factor. If, thereafter, we have a random system of selecting values for each factor from that distribution curve, a method of combining them to reach a DCF rate of return, and can calculate a sufficiently large number of individual solutions on the same basis, the DCF solutions can be ranged in such a way that the resulting rates of return will themselves form the pattern of a distribution curve of rates of return for the project.

Scope of Use of the Monte Carlo Technique

In a more complex project, for which uncertainty analysis is admirably suited, the analysis of the project may be carried much deeper than has previously been used in the DCF method of investment appraisal. So far, the method has used, as one of the factors to be appraised, the increase in annual income expected to result from the investment. This means there has been a clear-cut division between the roles played by the normal forecasting techniques and the DCF technique. In this way, the problem has been broken down into manageable proportions, each part of the problem being solved by the most appropriate technique, the DCF technique itself being employed solely to appraise the project in terms of the return that will be earned on the funds invested.

Where manual methods of appraisal are used, this approach has considerable merit. The bulk of the detailed work is carried out by what are for the most part well-understood techniques, and the unfamiliar technique (DCF) limited to what is a reasonably straightforward operation. The introduction of the computer in solving this type of problem permits a considerable extension of the volume of data and, in particular, variable data, that can be incorporated into the actual investment appraisal process.

Instead of starting the investment appraisal with a figure for the increase in revenue, for example, it may well start with the preliminary data upon which that increase was based. Each element in that data can then be evaluated independently. Such data may well include the volume of sales, variable costs, fixed costs, marketing costs, and so on. The calculation of values for these factors and the relationships between them is a normal analytical technique similar to that used in break-even analysis.

A number of the factors may be interrelated. The relationship between selling price, volume, and fixed and variable costs will be significant in determining the increase in profit that will be earned. When a computer is used and the DCF calculations start with these basic elements, the relationship between them can be incorporated in the computer program.

The cost factors themselves may be broken down into major categories each of which can be dealt with individually. The object of such a breakdown should be to highlight the critical areas of cost. Some of the cost factors are not likely to vary widely, or may not have a significant effect on the final result. Others may be subject to fairly wide fluctuations and have a significant effect upon the rate of return. These items, often called 'sensitive' costs, are those that should receive the closest attention throughout the appraisal stage and afterwards.

PROBABILITY ANALYSIS OF THE FACTORS USED

When all the factors to be used in the appraisal of a project have been segregated into subdivisions, a probability distribution curve covering the whole range of possible values for each must be prepared.

This may present problems, and, indeed, it sounds a formidable task. If it is approached in the right way, however, it should be possible to form a view of the probabilities of any particular value being achieved, this view bearing a close relationship to the actual case. By discussing each item with those people directly concerned, and by asking questions about the likelihood of different values being achieved, it should be possible to draw up a reasonably accurate picture of the distribution curve for that item.

123

Assume, for example, that the item for which we wish to draw up a distribution curve is the value of the sales revenue. Its value in the project has been forecast at £300 000 per annum. This is the most likely figure to be achieved, and what we want to know now is what are the probabilities that other values will be achieved. This could be ascertained by discussion with the sales and market research staff concerned with the project. Following a discussion of the project, we may well ask such questions as: 'Will the sales revenue ever exceed £500 000 or £450 000?'; 'Will it ever fall below £200 000?'; 'What are the chances that it will exceed £350 000, or be less than £260 000?' and so on.

After discussion and questioning, a pattern of the probability of different values being achieved should emerge, possibly on the following lines:

	£
Lower limit of sales revenue	220 000
There is a 4 per cent chance that it will be	240 000
There is a 6 per cent chance that it will be	275 000
There is a 10 per cent chance that it will be	290 000
There is a 45 per cent chance that it will be	300 000
There is a 20 per cent chance that it will be	340 000
There is a 10 per cent chance that it will be	375 000
There is a 5 per cent chance that it will be	400 000
Upper limit to sales revenue	440 000

These values can then be plotted to form the basis of a distribution curve for the sales revenue, which will show the possibilities of any individual value being achieved. The distribution curve would be as shown in Fig. 8.2.

This same approach is then applied to all the other factors used in the DCF calculation, and distribution curves drawn up for each. In the problem under consideration, the data has been broken down in the following way:

		£
Sales revenue	Most probable value	300 000
Material costs	Most probable value	50 000
Direct labour costs	Most probable value	75 000
Other variable costs	Most probable value	45 000
Fixed operating costs	Most probable value	70 000
Net cash investment	Most probable value	400 000
Residual value of plant, etc.	Most probable value	30 000
Life of project	Most probable value	10 years
Tax rate	Most probable value	40%
Capital allowances	No change expected	

Following detailed discussions with the staffs involved in the project, the distribution curves for each of the factors might appear as shown in Fig. 8.3.

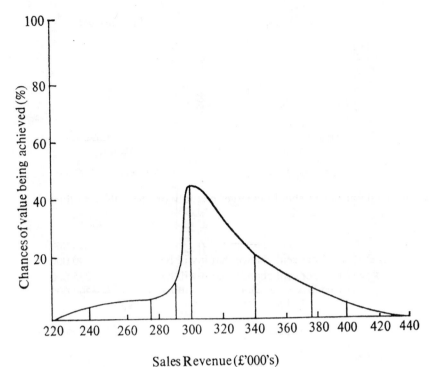

Sales Revenue (£'000's)

Figure 8.2. Distribution curve of possible value of sales revenue

COMPUTER OPERATION

The information given by each of the distribution curves is now translated into machine language and fed into the computer store. The computer now holds all the data relating to each of the factors to be used in evaluating the project, as well as the probability of any particular value being chosen for each item on a random selection. In addition, the computer holds the program that controls selection of the data and the calculation of a rate of return for each selection.

The computer is programmed to carry out enough selections from the data held in store to enable a sufficiently representative presentation of the distribution curve of the rate of return to be drawn. This may involve several hundred calculations of rates of return. Each selection will be made on a random basis, but the essential point is that the chances of any particular value being selected for any of the factors will depend entirely on the distribution curve of probability for that factor. In the end result, the number of times different values for a factor are chosen will correspond with the distribution curve that has been built up for that factor.

Each of the individual calculations will provide the rate of return for a particular selection, and during the running of the program the rates of return calculated all for the various selections will be accumulated and

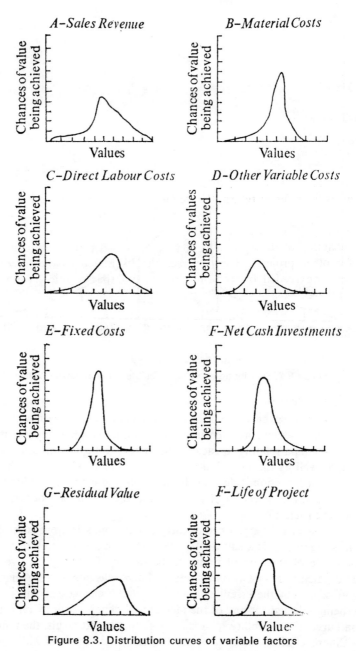

Figure 8.3. Distribution curves of variable factors

ranged in order of magnitude. At the end of the run, the number of times a particular rate of return has proved to be the solution rate, will provide the basis for the distribution curve of the probabilities of any rate being achieved for that project.

126

An example of the data used and solutions for a project is illustrated in Fig. 8.4 using the International Computers Ltd PROP (profit rating of projects) program. If required, this particular program provides for the use of periods of time less than one year which gives it greater flexibility.

Where risk analysis is wanted, the additional information required to operate the program consists of a percentage estimate of the probability of each cash flow element; the division of the ranges of cash flows into independently variable groups; and the number of runs required to provide an adequate sample.

When the full simulation of probabilities is used in the appraisal the computer output would be presented in the form shown in Fig. 8.5 (page 130). This gives the rates of return, the frequency of each rate being achieved and the cumulative frequency.

When considering a project, management now has a means of comparing the probability of different rates of return for that project with similar details for other projects. They can see the likelihood of the forecast rate achieved, or exceeded, or not being reached, and thus be able to form a much more rational judgement about the relative worth of a project than they could by merely considering a single rate of return. In Fig. 8.6 Project A is a much more desirable one than Project B, although the indicated rates of return are the same in both cases. A has a much higher probability of exceeding the forecast rate than B, and also has a lower probability of falling short of that rate.

Sensitivity Analysis

Management will frequently be concerned with what would happen to the rate of return in the event that forecast values for some of the factors incorporated in the appraisal prove to be under- or over-stated. For example, if the price level as a whole falls below the estimate or direct costs are underestimated. Here one would be dealing not with variables within the given range, but a change in the whole level of the range itself.

This is the type of effect that management would want to probe when appraising major projects. Where computer time is available the result in terms of changes in the rate of return can be assessed quite simply within the framework of values stored. Holding all other values constant, the values for the factor under review can be changed by the required amount and the effect on the rate of return noted.

A more formal system for assessing the sensitivity of the rate of return can be devised. In Fig. 8.7, it can be seen that, in the example illustrated, the most likely value for the rate of return is 10 per cent. If the value for factor A (let us say direct labour costs) is increased in value by 10 per cent, 20 per cent, and 30 per cent with all the other factors being held constant, the effect of these changes on the rate of return are seen at a^1, a^2,

ICL   PROP

PLANT EXPANSION - BRAND X.   ASSUMPTIONS - NO IN/DEFLATION OF COSTS/PRICES

GRANT 20%, ANNUAL ALL, 20%, REDUCING BALANCE FOR 5 YEARS, CORPORATION TAX 40%

YEAR	PERIOD	CAPITAL INVESTMENT	OTHER CAPITAL	INVESTMENT GRANT	INITIAL ALLOWANCE	ANNUAL ALLOWANCE	REVENUE INCOME	REVENUE COSTS	REVENUE PROFIT	TAX ON PROFIT	NET CASH FLOW
1970	3	-10000.0	0.0	0.0	0.0	0.0	0.0	-500.0	-500.0	0.0	-10500.0
	4	-2000.0	0.0	0.0	0.0	0.0	3000.0	-1000.0	2000.0	0.0	0.0
1971	1	0.0	0.0	0.0	0.0	0.0	2500.0	-1000.0	1500.0	0.0	1500.0
	2	0.0	0.0	0.0	0.0	0.0	2000.0	-1000.0	1000.0	0.0	1000.0
	3	0.0	0.0	0.0	0.0	640.0	3000.0	-1000.0	2000.0	-600.0	2040.0
	4	0.0	0.0	0.0	0.0	0.0	2500.0	-1000.0	1500.0	0.0	1500.0
1972	1	0.0	0.0	2000.00	0.0	0.0	2000.0	-1000.0	1000.0	0.0	3500.0
	2	0.0	0.0	0.0	0.0	0.0	2000.0	-1000.0	1000.0	0.0	1000.0
	3	0.0	0.0	0.0	0.0	512.0	3000.0	-1000.0	2000.0	-2400.0	112.0
	4	0.0	0.0	0.0	0.0	0.0	2500.0	-1500.0	1000.0	0.0	1000.0
1973	1	0.0	0.0	0.0	0.0	0.0	2000.0	-1500.0	500.0	0.0	1000.0
	2	0.0	0.0	0.0	0.0	0.0	2000.0	-1500.0	500.0	0.0	500.0
	3	0.0	0.0	0.0	0.0	409.6	2500.0	-1500.0	1000.0	-2200.0	500.0
	4	0.0	0.0	0.0	0.0	0.0	2500.0	-2000.0	500.0	0.0	-790.4
1974	1	0.0	0.0	0.0	0.0	0.0	0.0	0.0	0.0	0.0	500.0
	2	0.0	0.0	0.0	0.0	327.7	0.0	0.0	0.0	-1000.0	0.0
	3	0.0	0.0	0.0	0.0	0.0	0.0	0.0	0.0	0.0	-672.3
	4	0.0	0.0	0.0	0.0	0.0	0.0	0.0	0.0	0.0	0.0
1975	1	0.0	800.00	0.0	0.0	0.0	0.0	0.0	0.0	0.0	800.0
	2	0.0	0.0	0.0	0.0	0.0	0.0	0.0	0.0	0.0	0.0
	3	0.0	0.0	0.0	0.0	1310.7	0.0	0.0	0.0	0.0	1310.7
	4	0.0	0.0	0.0	0.0	0.0	0.0	0.0	0.0	0.0	0.0
1976	1	0.0	0.0	0.0	0.0	0.0	0.0	0.0	0.0	0.0	0.0
	2	0.0	0.0	0.0	0.0	0.0	0.0	0.0	0.0	0.0	0.0
	3	0.0	0.0	0.0	0.0	-320.0	0.0	0.0	0.0	0.0	-320.0

PLANT EXPANSION - BRAND X.   ASSUMPTIONS -   NO IN/DEFLATION OF COSTS/PRICES

GRANT 20%, ANNUAL ALL, 20%, REDUCING BALANCE FOR 5 YEARS, CORPORATION TAX 40%

D.C.F. YIELD RATE OF RETURN -   17.1886 %   PAYING RATE PER ANNUM, ACCURATE TO WITHIN 0.00001,   5.0000 % EARNING RATE

D.C.F. NET PRESENT VALUE OF PROJECT -   1702.1 AT   7.0000 % PAYING &   5.0000 % EARNING RATES PER ANNUM

D.C.F. NET PRESENT VALUE OF PROJECT -   1765.4 AT   7.0000 % PAYING &   4.0000 % EARNING RATES PER ANNUM

D.C.F. NET PRESENT VALUE OF PROJECT -   1634.0 AT   8.0000 % PAYING &   4.0000 % EARNING RATES PER ANNUM

PAYBACK PERIOD -   1 YEARS   3 PERIODS

AVERAGE ANNUAL RATE OF RETURN -   4.14 %

Notes on terms used:

DCF Yield Rate of return—Equivalent to the DCF rate of return used in this book.

Paying rate—The rate of interest the firm pays on borrowed capital.

Earning rate—The rate of interest the firm can expect to earn on surplus funds arising during the life of the project. The last two are used for a *dual-rate* calculation which avoids the possibility of a multiple rate solution. One of the rates is nominated and other is then resolved.

Figure 8.4. Project data and solution using the ICL profit rating of projects program

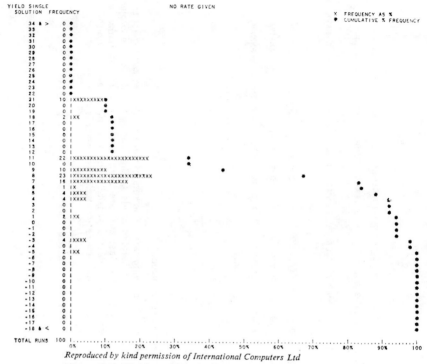

Reproduced by kind permission of International Computers Ltd

Figure 8.5. Yield random simulation printout and comments

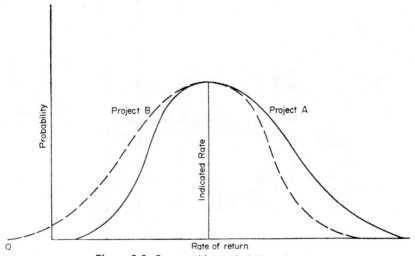

Figure 8.6. Comparable profitability of projects

130

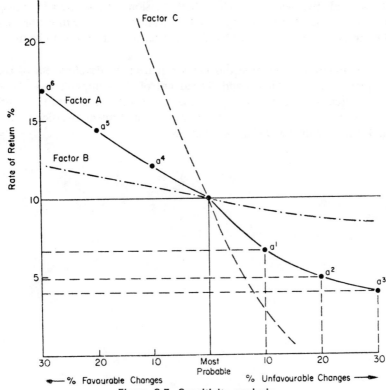

Figure 8.7. Sensitivity analysis

and a^3. If the values are then reduced by similar percentages, the resulting increases in the rate of return are shown at a^4, a^5, and a^6.

If the points a^1 to a^6 are now connected up by a curve, this will show the rate of return that would result from any percentage change in factor A within the limits illustrated. If the process is repeated and the results plotted on the chart in the same way for the other factors, the relative sensitivity of the rate of return to changes in any one of those factors is clearly seen. For example, the rate of return is much more sensitive to changes in factor C than for B.

This identification of relative sensitivity enables management to:

1. identify at the appraisal stage those elements in the project which require the closest scrutiny,
2. structure the control system when the project is operational, in a way that controls the sensitive factors much more closely,
3. decide where to probe in detail during the post audit.

As management becomes more scientific in its attitudes to problems, it will no longer accept the burden of making decisions without a quantitative

131

analysis of all the factors on which that decision is to be based. Management decisions today are largely based on techniques that will enable more and more of the factors involved in different business decisions to be quantified.

For the investment decision this has resulted in the development of DCF as a quantitative technique, and the advent of the computer has enabled this technique to be carried a stage further, so that it can be used to quantify the areas of uncertainty and risk in capital investment decisions, which should greatly reduce the element of chance.

9 Cost of Capital and Capital Budgeting

The Cost of Capital

The cost of capital to the business is directly influenced by the decisions of management regarding the way in which the long-term funds employed are raised. Most businesses of any size employ a combination of different types of funds, e.g., ordinary shares, retained profits, preference shares, borrowing, or, in unincorporated businesses, the owner's capital. The proportions in which these different sources of capital are used to meet the overall capital requirements of the business depends upon management's policy towards the owners of the business. As this aspect affects the corporate body much more than other classes of business ownership, it will be dealt with within the terms of the limited company.

The way in which a company raises its funds is a sphere of activity that has become remarkably fluid in recent years. The introduction of corporation tax in the United Kingdom changed attitudes towards borrowing money, so also has the development of recessional analysis techniques in the United States by Professor Donaldson* and others. Many businesses now undertake a fundamental reappraisal of the part debt financing plays in the corporate capital structure. Such trends can have a significant influence on the cost of capital to the company and deserve the closest attention when calculating a cost of capital factor for use in DCF.

MANAGEMENT *v.* SHAREHOLDERS

As managers of the business on behalf of the general body of shareholders, the board of directors should have two principal objectives in mind in relation to their financial policy. These objectives are:

1. To ensure that the return earned on the total long-term funds (or net assets) employed in the business is maintained at the maximum sustainable level.
2. To so arrange the way in which the long-term funds are raised that the long-term return to shareholders, both in income and capital appreciation, is maximized within given risk constraints.

* Gordon Donaldson, 'New Framework for Corporate Debt Policy', *Harvard Business Review*, March/April 1962, pp. 117–31.

DCF is intimately concerned with the first of these objectives. Each time it is proposed to take a proportion of the long-term funds and commit them to a specific use, DCF is used to measure the return that proportion of the funds should earn. This leads to a process of selection that should eliminate the less profitable projects.

The second of these objectives is not so directly related to DCF. The link between the two lies in the fact that the decisions taken in implementing the policy relating to this second objective will influence the cost of capital to the business. In this way, it will help to determine the cut-off or criterion rate of return used in the selection of projects.

GEARING

Raising funds by means of borrowing, rather than calling upon shareholders, adds to the risks of the business for the reasons outlined on page 101. The reward for taking those risks is the increase in the return to the ordinary shareholders—the gearing effect.

A simple illustration of the effect that gearing can have on the return on equity funds is given in Table 9.1, in which a new business requires the investment of £100 000 of long-term funds that should provide a return of £15 000 per year before tax. The figures in the table assume that two different methods of raising funds needed are available to the company. One relies entirely on obtaining funds from the ordinary shareholders, the other utilizes a combination of different sources of funds. The effect of 'gearing up' in the latter method is to more than double the return on the shareholders' funds.

TABLE 9.1. *Effect of Gearing on the Return to the Ordinary Shareholders*

All the capital provided by ordinary shareholders		Mixture of different sources of funds	
	£		£
Ordinary share capital	100 000	6% Debentures	40 000
		7% Preference shares	30 000
Profit before tax	15 000	Ordinary share capital	30 000
Corporation tax at 50%	7 500	Total capital	100 000
Profit available to			
ordinary shareholders	7 500	Profit before interest	
		and tax	15 000
		Debenture interest	2 400
		Profit before tax	12 60C
		Corporation tax at 50%	6 300
		Profit after tax	6 300
		Preference dividend net	1 470
		Profit available to	
		Ordinary shareholders	4 830
After tax return on equity 7·5%		After tax return on equity— $4\,830/30\,000 \times 100 = 16\cdot1\%$	

134

Management's policy towards maximizing the long-term values of the shareholders' interests will lead it to increase the proportion of the funds raised in the form of debt until it reaches a point where the increase in risk by further borrowing more than counterbalances the increase in return to the ordinary shareholders. Just where that point of balance will be depends upon the circumstances of each company. Property companies, which have almost their entire funds invested in land and buildings, will have a fairly stable income and adequate security, and thus will be able to fund a much higher proportion of their capital requirements by borrowing than a company operating in a volatile industry, where fluctuating profits make the risk of being unable to service their debt a very real one.

Gearing can, of course, benefit the shareholders but only if management can earn more on the total funds employed than it has to pay for the borrowed money. If the return earned on the total funds proves to be the same or less than that rate, then gearing will damage the interest of ordinary shareholders.

BALANCE BETWEEN DIFFERENT TYPES OF FUNDS

The importance of gearing from the point of view of DCF is that once management has defined its policy on the type and extent of gearing for the company the approximate proportion of each source of funds that will be used in future financing can be seen. This does not mean, however, that there will not be deviations from this norm. The raising of funds is not so precise an operation as that. Borrowing and raising funds from shareholders can normally be undertaken only in fairly large tranches, each of which will disturb the relationship in the short term. What it does mean is that over the long term, management will tend to move towards this 'normal' proportion even although the practical result will be a series of swings on either side of the norm. If the current fund raising is, say, in the form of a debenture, this may swing the proportion temporarily in favour of borrowing. The next fund raising, however, will most probably be in the form of equity funds, which will swing the balance, temporarily, the other way.

At the time of writing, the problem of what management should consider to be normal ratio between equity and borrowed funds is passing through a period of serious reappraisal because of the factors already outlined. The end result will be that debt becomes an instrument of financial policy rather than an expedient to meet a shortage of funds, and American trends in this respect are likely to be followed in Britain.

COST OF DIFFERENT SOURCES OF FUNDS

Given that the fundamental financing decision outlined above has been taken and that there are unlikely to be any further major changes in the basic relationship between borrowed and equity funds, it is possible to project an average cost of capital to the business. This will involve estimat-

135

ing the cost of each of the sources of capital used and calculating the weighted average cost for all the long-term funds employed in the business. The weights used for this purpose are the actual or prospective proportion of the funds derived from each of the sources. The cost factors will be a measure of the return that must be paid to the owners of the funds.

Borrowed Funds

The rate paid for the use of borrowed funds is capable of close estimation, since the rate is fixed and specified in the particulars of the issue. Taking corporation tax at 50 per cent, the after tax cost of an 8 per cent debenture is 4·0 per cent.

Shareholders' Funds

The position with shareholders' funds is not so straightforward. The cost of preference shares is not difficult to estimate since the rate of dividend is usually fixed and, when ACT is deducted, this is the cost to the company of this form of finance. With ordinary shares, however, the position is different. The equity funds comprise not only the nominal values of the ordinary shares that have been issued, but also the capital and revenue reserves. Moreover, the rate of dividend is not a measure of the return on the funds that can be used. The shareholder will not only be looking at the dividend paid to him each year; he will also take into account the backing this dividend receives in the form of earnings. Earnings retained in the business will influence the share value since they are expected to be invested in projects that will bring in a return and so increase the worth of the business.

A factor that will measure the cost of equity funds has to be decided on, taking into account the prospective levels of dividends and earnings and the influence they will have on the share value. Probably the closest approximation that can be made of this return is to consider the overall return that investors expect. If there are ample opportunities for investment offering yields of 10 per cent plus, then the prospective return offered by the company to new investors, calculated in such a way as that in Table 7.6, would have to equal that rate if the company wishes to attract new investment. This expected rate of return should provide a close approximation of the cost of equity funds.

There are more detailed methods of calculating the return on equity funds* and they require a close examination of the economic implications of raising new equity, but bearing in mind that we are dealing with marginal differences only, and that the cost of capital is only the starting point for deciding on the criterion rate of return, the cost factor for equity given by such a method should be close enough for practical purposes.

* See A. J. Merrett and Allen Sykes, *The Finance and Analysis of Capital Projects*, Longman, London, pp. 58–147.

Once the cost factors for all the sources of capital have been ascertained, they can be used to calculate the weighted average cost of the entire capital. The way in which this is done is shown in Table 9.2, which assumes that a company employs four different sources of funds, debentures, unsecured loan, preference shares, and ordinary shares. The proportion each of these sources provides is used as the basis for the weighting.

TABLE 9.2. *Calculation of the Weighted Average Cost of Capital*

Source of funds	Amount of funds	% of total	After tax cost	Weighted amount
	£	%	%	
7% Debentures	100 000	14·29	3·5	50·015
8% Unsecured loan	200 000	28·57	4·0	114·280
7% Preference shares	50 000	7·14	4·9	34·986
Ordinary share capital	200 000 ⎫			
Capital and revenue	⎬ 50·0	10·0	500·00	
reserves	150 000 ⎭			
	700 000	100·0		699·281
Weighted average cost of capital 6·993%				

AVERAGE OR MARGINAL COST OF CAPITAL

The question that will be asked at this stage is: should the weighted average cost of capital, as defined above, be used to calculate the criterion rate of return, or should the cost of the funds that will be employed to finance a particular project be used? In other words, should the average cost of capital or the marginal cost be used. If, for example, it is proposed to invest £1 million in a new project and this is to be financed by the issue of £1 million 7 per cent debentures, can we take the cost of the debentures as the cost of capital for this project?

The answer to this question lies in the way in which the company raises and uses the funds it employs. As was seen earlier, the company draws its funds from a number of different sources to provide a general pool of funds. Out of this general pool, it allocates amounts as and when required for projects. After an allocation, however, the funds employed on a project will in no way be identifiable with the particular source from which they were originally raised. Each source contributes to the general pool of funds available to the business, or what is usually called the capital employed. Out of this general pool management will allocate funds to specific projects. Whether the funds that are allocated to a particular project were originally raised by means of a debenture is purely fortuitous. It is impossible to point to a particular machine some time after it has been purchased and say 'That machine is financed by our 6 per cent debenture' because the identity of funds is lost as soon as they are brought into the general pool.

137

Even if it were possible to relate particular sources of funds with particular projects, it would not be right to relate the return on a project with the cost of the funds used to finance that project. If this were so, a project that gave an after tax return of 5 per cent would be accepted because it was financed by an 8 per cent unsecured loan (after tax cost 4·0 per cent), but later, a project that would give a return of 9 per cent would be rejected because it was financed by equity funds that had a cost of 10 per cent. Such an attitude would make nonsense of any system of investment appraisal.

In normal circumstances, therefore, the average weighted cost of capital is used as a base for the criterion rate of return, not the marginal cost of capital. As Hunt, Williams, and Donaldson* say,

> In order that a firm may avoid the dangers of becoming committed to certain investment opportunities with relatively low return to the exclusion of later opportunities offering a higher return, it is suggested that all investment opportunities should earn at least the weighted average cost of capital. It follows that each financing decision, whether it be to sell bonds, preferred stock, or common stock, or to retain earnings, will be regarded as one of a series that includes both debt and equity capital. At any point in time the current conditions of the market and the expectations as to future trends will determine the specific security to be used. If the market is judged accurately, this will keep the average cost of capital for the desired mix of sources at a minimum. In particular, the issuing company should aim to time its issues of high cost equity capital to coincide with periods of peak market prices, thus minimizing the number of shares issued.

There may be exceptional cases where the marginal cost of capital is appropriate. A property company may well raise finance that is specific to each project. Here, there is such a close relationship between the project and the way in which it is financed that it may be more appropriate to use the actual cost of the funds to be used. Similarly, if we are dealing with a specific investment overseas where political and economic considerations necessitate raising funds in a particular way, the cost of the actual funds raised might need to be considered.

Such cases must be dealt with on their merits, not losing sight of the effect the decision may have on the raising of funds for the rest of the company or group. In any case, a marginal rate that is less than the average should not be used since projects earning less than the average rate will lower the level of profitability of the business as a whole.

* Pearson Hunt, Charles M. Williams, Gordon Donaldson, *Basic Business Finance*, Richard D. Irwin, Homewood Ill, 1965, pp. 626–7.

Capital Budgeting

Once management has determined the cost of capital to the business, the next step is for it to determine the relationship that should exist between the cost of capital and the minimum rate of return that will be acceptable for investment projects.

The projects that compete for the available funds will include not only projects for which a rate of return can be measured, but also projects for which no rate of return can be calculated, but which it is essential that one should make. In the present social and economic conditions, most businesses find that funds must be employed to provide amenities of one sort or another for their employees. These may be essential if the firm is to continue to attract the personnel it requires from the locality.

In addition, the requirements of national legislation, local authority by-laws, insurance companies, etc., may necessitate improvements and additions to the premises and facilities of the firm if it is to continue in business. In all these cases the investment of funds is essential, but the return to the business is too intangible to be measured.

RELATIONSHIP BETWEEN THE COST OF CAPITAL AND CRITERION RATE OF RETURN

The cost of capital indicates the minimum acceptable return for the investment of funds *as a whole*. Some of the funds are committed to investments that earn no rate of return, and the bulk of the funds will be invested in projects for which a rate of return can be calculated. The minimum rate of return set for the latter class of project must be sufficient to provide the minimum rate of return on the total funds.

Example 9.1

The board of directors of Trelawny & Co. Ltd, are considering the allocation of funds for the following year. The proposals submitted for consideration are as shown in the first three columns of Table 9.3. The average cost of capital to the company after tax is $8\frac{1}{2}$ per cent.

Each of the projects included in Table 9.3 that has a rate of return, shows a return in excess of the cost of capital. The return on the proposed investments as a whole, however, falls below the cost of capital by 0·52 per cent. Clearly, if the schedule as a whole were to be approved the earnings from this combination of projects would fall below the cost of capital, and reduce profitability.

Management must define its policy towards the commitment of funds to non-earning projects, and decide what proportion of them it will devote to this purpose. Once defined, the basis of the criterion rate of return will be that the average return on the investments as a whole will exceed the cost of capital.

TABLE 9.3. *Capital Budget, Trelawny & Co. Ltd*

Item	Amount of funds required £	After tax return %	Weighted after tax return
Automatic conveyor system	100 000	10	1000
Lavatory block	36 000	nil	nil
Launch new product:			
Buildings	50 000		
Plant	62 000	⎱ ⎰ ς	1143
Working capital	15 000		
Replace delivery vehicles	10 000	8·5	85
New canteen	25 000	nil	nil
Machine replacement	110 000	9	990
Automatic packaging machine	9 000	12	108
Total	417 000		3326

Average return on projects 3326/417=7·98%

MORE THAN ONE CRITERION RATE OF RETURN

Management should also consider whether or not a single criterion rate should be used. The element of risk inherent in investment projects will vary greatly between one project and another. A project primarily based on definable costs' savings is obviously a smaller risk than that incurred in launching a new product.

Recognition of the difference in risk may be emphasized by classifying projects according to the amount of risk involved, and setting a different criterion rate for each class of project.

More directly the criterion rate may be related to the long-term rate of return set in the corporate objectives.

Inflation

Apart from short periods of time, the economies of countries all over the world have shown a continuous trend, in a greater or less degree, towards inflation. Such trends can have a significant effect on a business over the period of a capital investment project, and the effects will add further to the risks and uncertainties.

A number of the components of the cash flows will adjust to inflationary changes, depending upon the ability of the business to change its pricing and cost structure. The major factors incorporated in the net increase in income associated with a project will tend to adjust, more or less, with the changes in money values, and the sales revenue, wages and salaries, overheads, and so on, will do so within a relatively short time. Where long-term fixed-price contracts are taken, there will be a considerable delay in their adjustment.

The taxation reliefs related to the original capital expenditure will, however, continue to be allowed on the basis of the original money cost, and there will be no change in this factor. Unless management takes steps to adjust the value of its fixed assets, and adjusts its depreciation charges to a replacement value basis, the business will show a return on investment that is higher than the return in real values.

Work done by James P. Thrasher and Dr Rod Leach of McKinsey and Company Inc.* has shown that the effect of inflation on the return on investment can be severe. As an example, an investment in plant and machinery over a period of twenty years that shows a book return of 15 per cent, would have a return of only 10 per cent in real terms if inflation proceeds at 3 per cent per annum, and a return of only 7 per cent in real terms if inflation is at 6 per cent per annum.

TABLE 9.4. *Project with Large Property Element*

Net Cash Investment							£
Land and Buildings							50 000
Plant							50 000
							100 000

Year	Increase in profit before Deprecn.	Tax at 50%	Capital allowances	Tax saved	Cash flow	PV factors for 10%	Present value
1	6 000	—	30 000	15 000	21 000	0·909	19 089
2	6 000	3 000	5 000	2 500	5 500	0·826	4 543
3	6 000	3 000	3 750	1 875	4 875	0·751	3 661
4	6 000	3 000	2 812	1 406	4 406	0·683	3 009
5	6 000	3 000	2 109	1 054	4 054	0·621	2 517
6	6 000	3 000	1 582	791	3 791	0·564	2 138
7	6 000	3 000	1 187	593	3 593	0·513	1 843
8	6 000	3 000	890	445	3 445	0·467	1 609
9	4 000	3 000	667	334	1 334	0·424	566
10	4 000	2 000	501	251	2 251	0·386	868
11	—	2 000	—	—	(2 000)	0·350	(700)
	56 000	28 000	48 498	24 249	52 249		39 143
Residual Value							
Building £200 000							
Plant Nil							
Additional capital allowances			1 502	751	200 751	0·350	70 263
			50 000	25 000	253 000		109 406

In its appraisal of capital projects, in dealing with the inflation factor management must estimate its ability to adjust the cost and revenue of the business and the length of time it takes to achieve. Allowances will then have

* James P. Thrasher and Dr Rod Leach, 'Countering the hidden effects of inflation', *Financial Times*, 5 January 1967, p. 11.

to be made in the structure of the cash flows to take these changes into account.

A company can, of course, shift some of the burden of inflation on to lenders of money. Inflation erodes the real value of loans and reduces the real cost of eventual repayments of any loan. This is another argument for using debt in the capital structure.

A major point of difficulty may arise where land and buildings form a major part of the net cash investment. Because of their permanence, they lose little or none of their *real* value over the life of a project. Indeed, because of the effect of site scarcity, they may well increase in real value as well as money value, in which case they would add a large amount to the residual values. The large present value of residual items that would result may well make a project which has unprofitable underlying trading activities appear as an acceptable project.

In the illustration shown in Table 9.4, it can be seen that the project as a whole meets the criterion rate of 10 per cent. If, however, the values for the property are taken out the net cash investment becomes £50 000 and the total net present value £39 407 (109 407 less 200 000 × 0·350). The trading activity as such does not meet the criterion rate, but this has been obscured by the property values.

It follows that special care should be taken when any project with a large property element is under consideration. It is recommended that the property part of the project is taken out and appraised separately, leaving the trading element to be judged on its own merits.

Post-Audit

As with any other techniques based on planning and forecasting future operations, it is essential, if the quality of forecasting is to be maintained at a high level, that suitable methods should be evolved for checking the original forecasts against actual events. In many ways, of course, an overall view of trends can be obtained by comparing the rates of return earned on the capital employed. If a project coincides with an activity of the business that has a separate accounting system, as for example, where a division has been set up to manufacture and sell a new product, this may provide a simple way of checking the veracity of the forecasts. This is likely to be true in very few cases where DCF is used, and other methods must be considered.

Checking back on forecasts is often disliked in industry, but if it is known that there will be no check on the actual results, one of the principal factors that ensures accuracy in forecasting will be lost because the staff involved will know that their forecasts will not be challenged. If, on the other hand, staff know that the estimates used in building up the data for the project will be scrutinized after the project has been working for some time, they will be more careful in preparing them.

Apart from this aspect of the planning staff's activities, only by investigating the reasons for divergencies from forecasts can forecasting techniques be improved. The lessons learned from post-audit investigations can contribute considerably to the improvement of future forecasting techniques. Forecasting is, at best, an imprecise art, and every available opportunity for improving it should be seized.

SUITABLE PROJECTS

Not all projects will be susceptible to post-audit techniques, or indeed warrant them. Many financing decisions are based on values fixed by contract, and will not vary over the life of the project. Other projects may be small and integrated so closely with an operational activity of the business that there is little possibility of segregating the results of the investment decision from the operating results without considerable expenditure of time and effort. In such cases, selection of a sample of the projects for close attention should cover the needs for post-audit checks. If the profitability of one activity of the business falls, it may indicate the need for a fuller investigation of its capital investment programme.

For the larger project, which may form a significant proportion of an operational activity of the business, steps should be taken, as far as possible, to record the results flowing from that investment decision separately. As a very minimum, the recording of operating data for that activity should be arranged in such a way that the relevant data can be extracted from the records as and when required.

RESPONSIBILITY

As far as possible, the control of audit checks should not be the responsibility of the staff who originated the investment proposal. The group of people responsible for carrying them out may include members of the capital budgeting team so as to derive the benefit of their particular expertise, and to provide a quick feedback to the capital budgeting department. The audit group, as such, should, however, have direct responsibility to management at a higher level than the head of the budgeting department.

TIMING

With smaller investment projects the post-audit check should take place some twelve to eighteen months after the investment has been made. The precise timing will depend upon the complexity and time scale of the project. The check should take place as soon as possible after the project has settled down in its final operating form, so that the feedback of information can take place quickly.

The more complex project, in which the time occupied by constructional

143

work may be considerable, and followed by a lengthy build-up to full operating capacity, presents a different problem. In this, post-audit checks should be made at different stages of the project, i.e., completion of construction, early operating level, final operating level. If the check is left until the project is operating at planned capacity, it may be several years before the lessons learned from that project can be incorporated in future planning techniques.

COMPENSATING FOR MANAGERIAL BIAS

Some managers have a bias towards pessimism when making forecasts, others an optimistic one. A post-audit record of the outcome of each manager's forecasts may help to identify these traits. It may then be possible to build in to the appraisal system factors to correct such bias.

Conclusions

At the beginning of this book, emphasis was laid upon the need for managers to be more concerned with the profitability of the businesses they manage. This was not emphasized with the object of focusing their attention solely upon the rewards that might accrue to them personally. Individuals should rightly be concerned with returns to them personally, but the objective in increasing profitability should go beyond such rewards.

In the one-man business profitability and personal return go hand in hand, since the profit earned by the business will be reflected directly in personal income. In the larger business this direct link will not be so discernable. The individual's remuneration may well be linked with the prosperity of that part of the business that he manages, but the cause and effect relationship between the two is not always seen to be so close.

The higher levels of management in the corporate structure may not always want any close connection between the profitability of the business they manage and their own return. The rise to eminence of the professional manager has tended to cut across the link between the providers of risk capital and the businesses they have helped to finance. Often, managements consider themselves to be, not the representatives of the owners of the business but a body in their own right who have responsibilities to 'their' employees, to the State, and to the community at large. All too often these responsibilities are taken to be more important than their responsibilities to the owners of the business.

It is right that management should bear in mind that the business does have responsibilities to people other than shareholders. The standing of the business in the community may have a real bearing upon its future progress. The danger is that this division may obscure the relevance and importance of the profitability of the business. This danger is not only the narrow one that it may limit or reduce the return to the owners of the business, but also the wider implication that it may have for the economy as a whole.

Shareholders will be vitally concerned with the return that can be earned on the funds they have provided for the business. Their capacity to save and provide funds for future investment, as well as their level of income, will be conditional on the return that can be earned on current investments, whether such savings are made compulsorily through company retentions, or by individual voluntary effort.

The implications of profitability, however, go beyond the interests of the individual. In the long run, the company that achieves a high level of profitability will be the one that is in the best position to improve the rewards to the people it employs, and to provide the backing for future capital investment. The profitable firm is the one that is in a position to examine and introduce reductions in the price of the goods or services that it provides, and so promote the long-term welfare of the business itself. The profitable business is the one that provides the resources necessary for the proper running of the machinery of state through its contributions to the tax revenue of the country. In short, the more a business produces over and above the resources it employs, the better will it be able to contribute to the general advancement of the country.

This may be considered to be special pleading for the private enterprise economy, and, of course, in the context of the words used, it is. But what has been said about profitability applies equally to any socialistic economy. Only if the resources committed to business operations, however organized, are employed profitably, will the economy as a whole prosper. If a state-owned industry produces a commodity that is not wanted by the public it is not contributing to the wealth of that country, but is, in fact, consuming it. In the private enterprise system, the firm makes a loss, in the state-owned system it makes a negative contribution to the country's economy.

If, then, profitability is of the utmost importance to the progress of a nation, it is right that management should be educated to use profitability as a much more stringent measurement of their efficiency than heretofore. If managements are more aware that they will be judged by such a yardstick, then they will be searching for techniques that will provide them, in turn, with a yardstick for measuring the effect their decisions may have when committing the funds of the business to new uses. Such a yardstick is provided by DCF. It enables management to measure the rate of return likely to be earned on projects, and, in some measure, to quantify the risks and uncertainties that may be present.

The measure of profitability of the business as a whole is the return it earns on the capital employed. Within individual businesses capital employed is represented by a particular combination of net assets, which is a result of investment decisions in the past. The significance of DCF is that it will, in a major way, influence the future disposition of funds among the various

145

assets resulting from current decisions. Its major impact will, of course, be in assessing the return on fixed assets, but we must not ignore the fact that once a certain disposition of funds has been made, and assets committed to a particular course of action, decisions on the use of working capital can be made only within the existing framework.

The use of DCF within the framework of the general allocation of funds will, therefore, decisively affect the return that can be earned on the capital employed, and the quality of the decisions made by management will be directly reflected in that return.

DCF, then, has an important role to play in the decision-making process of any organization. It must not, however, be elevated to an importance to which it does not aspire. It will be at all times subservient to the policy formulation of senior management, and can only be used to further the implementation of that policy. It is not a policy-making instrument; it is only a technique. But it is a technique that will enable management to quantify the possible results of their decisions in such a way that rational decisions based on the widest degree of information possible can be made.

Appendix A. Present Value of £1 Receivable at the End of Each Period

Year	Percentage									
	1	2	3	4	5	6	7	8	9	10
1	0·990	0·980	0·971	0·962	0·952	0·943	0·935	0·926	0·917	0·909
2	0·980	0·961	0·943	0·925	0·907	0·890	0·873	0·857	0·842	0·826
3	0·971	0·942	0·915	0·889	0·864	0·840	0·816	0·794	0·772	0·751
4	0·961	0·924	0·888	0·855	0·823	0·792	0·763	0·735	0·708	0·683
5	0·951	0·906	0·863	0·822	0·784	0·747	0·713	0·681	0·650	0·621
6	0·942	0·888	0·837	0·790	0·746	0·705	0·666	0·630	0·596	0·564
7	0·933	0·871	0·813	0·760	0·711	0·665	0·623	0·583	0·547	0·513
8	0·923	0·853	0·789	0·731	0·677	0·627	0·582	0·540	0·502	0·467
9	0·914	0·837	0·766	0·703	0·645	0·592	0·544	0·500	0·460	0·424
10	0·905	0·820	0·744	0·676	0·614	0·558	0·508	0·463	0·422	0·386
11	0·896	0·804	0·722	0·650	0·585	0·527	0·475	0·429	0·388	0·350
12	0·887	0·788	0·701	0·625	0·557	0·497	0·444	0·397	0·356	0·319
13	0·879	0·773	0·681	0·601	0·530	0·469	0·415	0·368	0·326	0·290
14	0·870	0·758	0·661	0·577	0·505	0·442	0·388	0·340	0·299	0·263
15	0·861	0·743	0·642	0·555	0·481	0·417	0·362	0·315	0·275	0·239
16	0·853	0·728	0·623	0·534	0·458	0·394	0·339	0·292	0·252	0·218
17	0·844	0·714	0·605	0·513	0·436	0·371	0·317	0·270	0·231	0·198
18	0·836	0·700	0·587	0·494	0·416	0·350	0·296	0·250	0·212	0·180
19	0·828	0·686	0·570	0·475	0·396	0·331	0·277	0·232	0·194	0·164
20	0·820	0·673	0·554	0·456	0·377	0·312	0·258	0·215	0·178	0·149
21	0·811	0·660	0·538	0·439	0·359	0·294	0·242	0·199	0·164	0·135
22	0·803	0·647	0·522	0·422	0·342	0·278	0·226	0·184	0·150	0·123
23	0·795	0·634	0·507	0·406	0·326	0·262	0·211	0·170	0·138	0·112
24	0·788	0·622	0·492	0·390	0·310	0·247	0·197	0·158	0·126	0·102
25	0·780	0·610	0·478	0·375	0·295	0·233	0·184	0·146	0·116	0·092
30	0·742	0·552	0·412	0·308	0·231	0·174	0·131	0·099	0·075	0·057
35	0·706	0·500	0·355	0·253	0·181	0·130	0·094	0·068	0·049	0·036
40	0·672	0·453	0·307	0·208	0·142	0·097	0·067	0·046	0·032	0·022

Year	Percentage									
	11	12	13	14	15	16	17	18	19	20
1	0·901	0·893	0·885	0·877	0·870	0·862	0·855	0·847	0·840	0·833
2	0·812	0·797	0·783	0·769	0·756	0·743	0·731	0·718	0·706	0·694
3	0·731	0·712	0·693	0·675	0·658	0·641	0·624	0·609	0·593	0·579
4	0·659	0·636	0·613	0·592	0·572	0·552	0·534	0·516	0·499	0·482
5	0·593	0·567	0·543	0·519	0·497	0·476	0·456	0·437	0·419	0·402
6	0·535	0·507	0·480	0·456	0·432	0·410	0·390	0·370	0·352	0·335
7	0·482	0·452	0·425	0·400	0·376	0·354	0·333	0·314	0·296	0·279
8	0·434	0·404	0·376	0·351	0·327	0·305	0·285	0·266	0·249	0·233
9	0·391	0·361	0·333	0·308	0·284	0·263	0·243	0·225	0·209	0·194
10	0·352	0·322	0·295	0·270	0·247	0·227	0·208	0·191	0·176	0·162
11	0·317	0·287	0·261	0·237	0·215	0·195	0·178	0·162	0·148	0·135
12	0·286	0·257	0·231	0·208	0·187	0·168	0·152	0·137	0·124	0·112
13	0·258	0·229	0·204	0·182	0·163	0·145	0·130	0·116	0·104	0·093
14	0·232	0·205	0·181	0·160	0·141	0·125	0·111	0·099	0·088	0·078
15	0·209	0·183	0·160	0·140	0·123	0·108	0·095	0·084	0·074	0·065
16	0·188	0·163	0·141	0·123	0·107	0·093	0·081	0·071	0·062	0·054
17	0·170	0·146	0·125	0·108	0·093	0·080	0·069	0·060	0·052	—
18	0·153	0·130	0·111	0·095	0·081	0·069	0·059	0·051	—	—
19	0·138	0·116	0·098	0·083	0·070	0·060	0·051	—	—	—
20	0·124	0·104	0·087	0·073	0·061	0·051	—	—	—	—
21	0·112	0·093	0·077	0·064	0·053	—	—	—	—	—
22	0·101	0·083	0·068	0·056	—	—	—	—	—	—
23	0·091	0·074	0·060	—	—	—	—	—	—	—
24	0·082	0·066	0·053	—	—	—	—	—	—	—
25	0·074	0·059	—	—	—	—	—	—	—	—

Year	Percentage									
	21	22	23	24	25	26	27	28	29	30
1	0·826	0·820	0·813	0·806	0·800	0·794	0·787	0·781	0·775	0·769
2	0·683	0·672	0·661	0·650	0·640	0·630	0·620	0·610	0·601	0·592
3	0·564	0·551	0·537	0·524	0·512	0·500	0·488	0·477	0·466	0·455
4	0·467	0·451	0·437	0·423	0·410	0·397	0·384	0·373	0·361	0·350
5	0·386	0·370	0·355	0·341	0·328	0·315	0·303	0·291	0·280	0·269
6	0·319	0·303	0·289	0·275	0·262	0·250	0·238	0·227	0·217	0·207
7	0·263	0·249	0·235	0·222	0·210	0·198	0·188	0·178	0·168	0·159
8	0·218	0·204	0·191	0·179	0·168	0·157	0·148	0·139	0·130	0·123
9	0·180	0·167	0·155	0·144	0·134	0·125	0·116	0·108	0·101	0·094
10	0·149	0·137	0·126	0·116	0·107	0·099	0·092	0·085	0·078	0·073
11	0·123	0·112	0·103	0·094	0·086	0·079	0·072	0·066	0·061	0·056
12	0·102	0·092	0·083	0·076	0·069	0·062	0·057	0·052	—	—
13	0·084	0·075	0·068	0·061	0·055	—	—	—	—	—
14	0·069	0·062	0·055	—	—	—	—	—	—	—
15	0·057	0·051	—	—	—	—	—	—	—	—

Appendix B. Present Value of £1 Receivable Annually at the End of Each Year

					Percentage					
Year	1	2	3	4	5	6	7	8	9	10
1	0·990	0·980	0·971	0·962	0·952	0·943	0·935	0·926	0·917	0·909
2	1·970	1·942	1·913	1·886	1·859	1·833	1·808	1·783	1·759	1·736
3	2·941	2·884	2·829	2·775	2·723	2·673	2·624	2·577	2·531	2·487
4	3·902	3·808	3·717	3·630	3·546	3·465	3·387	3·312	3·240	3·170
5	4·853	4·713	4·580	4·452	4·329	4·212	4·100	3·993	3·890	3·791
6	5·795	5·601	5·417	5·242	5·076	4·917	4·767	4·623	4·486	4·355
7	6·728	6·472	6·230	6·002	5·786	5·582	5·389	5·206	5·033	4·868
8	7·652	7·325	7·020	6·733	6·463	6·210	5·971	5·747	5·535	5·335
9	8·566	8·162	7·786	7·435	7·108	6·802	6·515	6·247	5·995	5·759
10	9·471	8·983	8·530	8·111	7·722	7·360	7·024	6·710	6·418	6·145
11	10·368	9·787	9·253	8·760	8·306	7·887	7·499	7·139	6·805	6·495
12	11·255	10·575	9·954	9·385	8·863	8·384	7·943	7·536	7·161	6·814
13	12·134	11·348	10·635	9·986	9·394	8·853	8·358	7·904	7·487	7·103
14	13·004	12·106	11·296	10·563	9·899	9·295	8·745	8·244	7·786	7·367
15	13·865	12·849	11·938	11·118	10·380	9·712	9·108	8·559	8·061	7·606
16	14·718	13·578	12·561	11·652	10·838	10·106	9·447	8·851	8·313	7·824
17	15·562	14·292	13·166	12·166	11·274	10·477	9·763	9·122	8·544	8·022
18	16·398	14·992	13·754	12·659	11·690	10·828	10·059	9·372	8·756	8·201
19	17·226	15·678	14·324	13·134	12·085	11·158	10·336	9·604	8·950	8·365
20	18·046	16·351	14·877	13·590	12·462	11·470	10·594	9·818	9·129	8·514
21	18·857	17·011	15·415	14·029	12·821	11·764	10·836	10·017	9·292	8·649
22	19·660	17·658	15·937	14·451	13·163	12·042	11·061	10·201	9·442	8·772
23	20·456	18·292	16·444	14·857	13·489	12·303	11·272	10·371	9·580	8·883
24	21·243	18·914	16·936	15·247	13·799	12·550	11·469	10·529	9·707	8·985
25	22·023	19·523	17·413	15·622	14·094	12·783	11·654	10·675	9·823	9·077
30	25·808	22·396	19·600	17·292	15·372	13·765	12·409	11·258	10·274	9·427
35	29·409	24·999	21·487	18·665	16·374	14·498	12·948	11·655	10·567	9·644
40	32·835	27·355	23·115	19·793	17·159	15·046	13·332	11·925	10·757	9·779

					Percentage					
Year	11	12	13	14	15	16	17	18	19	20
1	0·901	0·893	0·885	0·877	0·870	0·862	0·855	0·847	0·840	0·833
2	1·713	1·690	1·668	1·647	1·626	1·605	1·585	1·566	1·546	1·528
3	2·444	2·402	2·361	2·322	2·283	2·246	2·210	2·174	2·140	2·106
4	3·102	3·037	2·974	2·914	2·855	2·798	2·743	2·690	2·639	2·589
5	3·696	3·605	3·517	3·433	3·352	3·274	3·199	3·127	3·058	2·991
6	4·231	4·111	3·998	3·889	3·784	3·685	3·589	3·498	3·410	3·326
7	4·712	4·564	4·423	4·288	4·160	4·039	3·922	3·812	3·706	3·605
8	5·146	4·968	4·799	4·639	4·487	4·344	4·207	4·078	3·954	3·837
9	5·537	5·328	5·132	4·946	4·772	4·607	4·451	4·303	4·163	4·031
10	5·889	5·650	5·426	5·216	5·019	4·833	4·659	4·494	4·339	4·192
11	6·207	5·938	5·687	5·453	5·234	5·029	4·836	4·656	4·486	4·327
12	6·492	6·194	5·918	5·660	5·421	5·197	4·988	4·793	4·610	4·439
13	6·650	6·424	6·122	5·842	5·583	5·342	5·118	4·910	4·715	4·533
14	6·982	6·628	6·302	6·002	5·724	5·468	5·229	5·008	4·802	4·611
15	7·191	6·811	6·462	6·142	5·847	5·575	5·324	5·092	4·876	4·675
16	7·379	6·974	6·604	6·265	5·954	5·669	5·405	5·162	4·938	4·730
17	7·549	7·120	6·729	6·373	6·047	5·749	5·475	5·222	4·990	4·775
18	7·702	7·250	6·840	6·467	6·128	5·818	5·534	5·273	5·033	4·812
19	7·839	7·366	6·938	6·550	6·198	5·877	5·584	5·316	5·070	4·844
20	7·963	7·469	7·025	6·623	6·259	5·929	5·628	5·353	5·101	4·870
21	8·075	7·562	7·102	6·687	6·312	5·973	5·665	5·384	5·127	4·891
22	8·176	7·645	7·170	6·743	6·359	6·011	5·696	5·410	5·149	4·909
23	8·266	7·718	7·230	6·792	6·399	6·044	5·723	5·432	5·167	4·925
24	8·348	7·784	7·283	6·835	6·434	6·073	5·746	5·451	5·182	4·937
25	8·422	7·843	7·330	6·873	6·464	6·097	5·766	5·467	5·195	4·948
30	8·694	8·055	7·496	7·003	6·566	6·177	5·829	5·517	5·235	4·979
35	8·855	8·175	7·586	7·070	6·617	6·215	5·858	5·539	5·251	4·992
40	8·951	8·244	7·634	7·105	6·642	6·234	5·871	5·548	5·258	4·997

Year	Percentage									
	21	22	23	24	25	26	27	28	29	30
1	0·826	0·820	0·813	0·806	0·800	0·794	0·787	0·781	0·775	0·769
2	1·509	1·492	1·474	1·457	1·440	1·424	1·407	1·392	1·376	1·361
3	2·074	2·042	2·011	1·981	1·952	1·923	1·896	1·868	1·842	1·816
4	2·540	2·494	2·448	2·404	2·362	2·320	2·280	2·241	2·203	2·166
5	2·926	2·864	2·803	2·745	2·689	2·635	2·583	2·532	2·483	2·436
6	3·245	3·167	3·092	3·020	2·951	2·885	2·821	2·759	2·700	2·643
7	3·508	3·416	3·327	3·242	3·161	3·083	3·009	2·937	2·868	2·802
8	3·726	3·619	3·518	3·421	3·329	3·241	3·156	3·076	2·999	2·925
9	3·905	3·786	3·673	3·566	3·463	3·366	3·273	3·184	3·100	3·019
10	4·054	3·923	3·799	3·682	3·571	3·465	3·364	3·269	3·178	3·092
11	4·177	4·035	3·902	3·776	3·656	3·544	3·437	3·335	3·239	3·147
12	4·278	4·127	3·985	3·851	3·725	3·606	3·493	3·387	3·286	3·190
13	4·362	4·203	4·053	3·912	3·780	3·656	3·538	3·427	3·322	3·223
14	4·432	4·265	4·108	3·962	3·824	3·695	3·573	3·459	3·351	3·249
15	4·489	4·315	4·153	4·001	3·859	3·726	3·601	3·483	3·373	3·268
16	4·536	4·357	4·189	4·033	3·887	3·751	3·623	3·503	3·390	3·283
17	4·576	4·391	4·219	4·059	3·910	3·771	3·640	3·518	3·403	3·295
18	4·608	4·419	4·243	4·080	3·928	3·786	3·654	3·529	3·413	3·304
19	4·635	4·442	4·263	4·097	3·942	3·799	3·664	3·539	3·421	3·311
20	4·657	4·460	4·279	4·110	3·954	3·808	3·673	3·546	3·427	3·316
21	4·675	4·476	4·292	4·121	3·963	3·816	3·679	3·551	3·432	3·320
22	4·690	4·488	4·302	4·130	3·970	3·822	3·684	3·556	3·436	3·323
23	4·703	4·499	4·311	4·137	3·976	3·827	3·689	3·559	3·438	3·325
24	4·713	4·507	4·318	4·143	3·981	3·831	3·692	3·562	3·441	3·327
25	4·721	4·514	4·323	4·147	3·985	3·834	3·694	3·564	3·442	3·329
30	4·746	4·534	4·339	4·160	3·995	3·842	3·701	3·569	3·447	3·332
35	4·756	4·541	4·345	4·164	3·998	3·845	3·703	3·571	3·448	3·333
40	4·760	4·544	4·347	4·166	3·999	3·846	3·703	3·571	3·448	3·333

Appendix C

Depreciation and Cash Flow

There are a number of misunderstandings about the relationship between depreciation and cash flow. It is included in the cash flows as defined in this book, but, at the same time, we say that there is no cash flow for depreciation since it is only a book entry. Others argue that depreciation does not determine cash flow on the grounds that if the basis for depreciation is changed it does not alter the amount of the cash flow.

To clear up this point, consider the following example. A company is set up to own and operate one machine. The balance sheet at the start of the enterprise is shown at A. All the trading periods are rolled up into one accounting period so that the machine is fully depreciated in that period. The profit and loss account for the period's trading is shown in B.

At the end of the accounting period the balance sheet would appear as shown in C (assuming that there are no debtors or creditors). The cash balance of £120 is derived from the difference between the cash income from sales and those expenses requiring a cash outlay.

The *cash flow* is the difference between the cash inflow from sales and what we could call the 'cash' expenses. In *accounting terms* this cash flow

A. Balance Sheet at Commencement

	£		£
Share Capital	100	Machine	100

B. Profit and Loss Account for the Trading Period

	£
Sales	200
Less:	
Expenses other than Depreciation	80
Depreciation	100
Net Profit	20

C. Closing Balance Sheet

	£		£
Share Capital	100	Machine	100
Net Profit	20	*Less* Depreciation	100
			—
		Cash	120
	120		120

is then divided into depreciation and profit. If, for example, it was now decided to spread the depreciation over two accounting periods rather than one, it would not affect the cash flow. All it would do is to divide the cash flow into different amounts for depreciation and profit. In the example they would change to £50 depreciation and £70 profit, with the cash flow remaining at £120.

Checklist

Below is a checklist of major points that must be dealt with if the capital investment decision process is to be effective.

1. LONG-RANGE PLANNING DECISIONS
   (a) Define and quantify the pattern of long-term investment required to achieve the corporate goals.
   (b) What mix of funds is to be used and the likely cost?
   (c) Group types of investment by risk classification.
   (d) Set overall long-term return required from new investments.
   (e) Set minimum rate of return criteria for different risk groups.
   (f) Decide how inflation will be taken into account.

2. SETTING THE PROJECT FRAMEWORK
   (a) Define objective of the proposal.
   (b) Ensure that all alternatives are considered.
   (c) Discard any alternatives which are clearly not viable.
   (d) Quantify the consequences of all alternatives that can be quantified in money terms.
   (e) Detail all non-quantifiable consequences.
   (f) Set time horizon for project and for each alternative for the project.

3. VOLUME AND TIMING OF CASH FLOWS
   (a) Setting up the project:
       (i) Cost of new buildings and machinery.
       (ii) Cash value of any existing machines that will be used and which otherwise would be sold.
       (iii) Working capital.
       (iv) Marketing costs.
       (v) Commissioning or running in costs.
       (vi) Existing plant that will be sold.
       (vii) Any tax consequences of each of the above.
       (viii) Any grants, etc., which might be received from state or local governments.

153

(b) Operations:
     (i) Extra income and expenses (excluding depreciation) arising from the project.
     (ii) Cost savings.
     (iii) Any exceptional items not included above.
     (iv) The tax consequences of the above.
(c) Residual values:
     (i) Realizable value of buildings, plant, and equipment.
     (ii) Release of working capital.
     (iii) Any terminal outlays, e.g., restoration costs.
     (iv) Tax consequences of the above.

4. TAXATION

(a) Rate of tax.

(b) Any time delay after earnings before tax must be paid.

(c) Are corporate profits large enough to enable the cash benefit of capital allowances to be taken at the earliest possible date?

(d) Are they large enough to allow tax relief on early losses in running the project to be taken?

(e) If corporate profits are not large enough in the above two cases, then how long will it be before the appropriate reliefs can be taken?

(f) Can any grants towards the cost of buildings and plant be claimed?

(g) Does the government of the country in which the project will be situated allow a 'tax holiday' for new projects?

(h) What is the appropriate method of claiming capital allowances to give the higher present value?

(j) Where plant will be disposed of what will be the written down values and what will be the tax consequences?

(k) Are there any grants towards the training of staff, etc.?

5. SEEKING ALTERNATIVES

(a) Have all possible methods of achieving the objective of the project been considered?

(b) Will operating in a different part of the country or abroad bring tax or other advantages which outweigh any disadvantages?

(c) Does the rate of return on each incremental slice of investment, where a series of alternatives are being considered, meet the minimum rate of return criteria and exceed the rate that can be earned on other investments?

(d) Has the possibility of leasing been considered?

154

(*e*) If so, what are the net rental values and other incremental cash flows?

6. ORGANIZATIONAL

   (*a*) Is long-range planning organized in a way that provides the answers to poirts raised at 1 above?
   (*b*) Have adequate guidelines been provided for line managers to help them formulate projects and avoid wasted effort?
   (*c*) Is there a vetting system that ensures that projects are adequately probed and tested before submission for approval?
   (*d*) Is adequate financial and technical advice available to people originating project proposals?
   (*e*) Is the capital budget committee properly briefed as to the long-term requirements of the business and of the profitability criteria adopted?
   (*f*) Is the post-audit adequate?
   (*g*) Is there adequate feedback from the post-audit to give adequate checks on forecasting?

7. OTHER

   (*a*) Inflation:
      (i) Is management aware of likely trends?
      (ii) How quickly can prices be adjusted?
      (iii) Can the burden be shifted to others through long-term borrowing?
      (iv) What are the major factors in the projected affected by inflation?
   (*b*) Does the profit pattern resulting from the most profitable mix of projects provide an acceptable level of profit reporting at all times, or will there be periods where reported corporate profits will be so low as to adversely affect share price?

Problems

Below is a selection of problems which can be used to test one's understanding of the use of DCF. Model solutions are provided on page 159. These are based upon certain assumptions of timing, etc., and it should be borne in mind that alternative assumptions might be available.

1. You can purchase the reversionary interest under a will for £2500. An examination of the life expectancy tables indicates that it is likely to fall in in 20 years' time. The value of the interest is £16 000. If you can earn a net return of 10 per cent on money under your own management is this a good purchase?

2. You have been quoted a price of £9500 for a machine which you estimate will save you £1500 per year net of tax and benefits of capital allowances for a period of 15 years. The machine would be worthless at the end of this period. The business offers other opportunities of earning 12 per cent on funds invested. Would you purchase the machine?

3. The production manager proposes to purchase a machine at a cost of £15 000. Installation and carriage costs are estimated at £600. He estimates that it will save labour and material costs of £3000 in the first year and £5000 per year for each of the remaining four years of its life. Currently you are able to claim a first-year allowance of 60 per cent on new plant. At the end of the five years, the plant will have no value. The rate of corporation tax is 50 per cent. Management aims at earning a minimum rate of return of 10 per cent on all projects. (a) Compute the rate of return. (b) Using 10 per cent as the criterion rate, compute the profitability index.

4. Graffham and Co. Ltd are a very profitable company. However, one of the products in the consumer field is becoming very dated. It is proposed to replace this with a new, improved, product. Estimates of the likely level of sales and costs for the new product indicate that the increase in profits before depreciation would be £10 000 in the first year and £25 000 in subsequent years. The costs included in that estimate do not allow for the fact that marketing costs of £10 000 would be allowed for in the first year.

New plant will be required having a cost of approximately £110 000 and will be installed during the year prior to the launch of the new product and is expected to have a working life of ten years. At the end of that period, its scrap value will be of the order of £5000. Existing plant having a realizable value of £2000 and a written down value for tax purposes of £1000 will be sold as a result of the decision.

The current tax rate is 50 per cent and the company would be able to claim 100 per cent first-year allowances, if it so desires.

On the forecast level of sales, it is estimated that an additional £15 000 working capital would be required in the year of launching the product and a further £10 000 in the following year.

What is the rate of return on the project?

5. Assume that the management of Graffham and Co. Ltd have decided to proceed with the project outlined in question 4. A leasing company have been approached to see whether or not they would acquire the plant and equipment and lease it to Graffham. For this they have quoted a yearly rental for the ten years of £15 000 per year and if it is retained after this period the rental will be reduced to a nominal figure. At the same time the leasing company would assume some of the ownership costs of the plant estimated at £1000 per year.

There are ample opportunities within Graffham and Co. Ltd for investment in projects with returns in excess of 10 per cent after tax.

Should the company lease the equipment or purchase it outright?

6. The Board of Directors of the A. B. Mining Co. Ltd are considering erecting a smelter on an overseas mining site at a cost of £1·5 million. The ability to process their own ore is expected to add £300 000 per year to profits net of local tax and the benefits of capital allowances. The ore body has an estimated life of nine years. A state grant of £300 000 would be receivable in the year after completion.

During the course of the discussions the company's Chief Engineer has proposed erecting an even more sophisticated smelter which, because the metal would be more pure as a result, would add £350 000 to profits net of tax, etc., rather than the £300 000 in the original proposal. The cost of this investment would be £1·9m less £400 000 grant. The company has plenty of investment opportunities which would offer returns in excess of 12 per cent.

The company's adviser believes that the project would not add to the United Kingdom tax payable. Restoration costs would cover any realizable value of the plant at the end of nine years.

Because of uncertainties in the metal price, the board wish to see whether the relative values of the two versions of the smelter would change if declining metal prices reduced the net return by £80 000 in each year.

7. The Finance Committee of the Board of Directors of Van Diemen Ltd are currently considering which of two loan proposals to accept. One proposal involves raising £2 million at 8·75 per cent interest, with the loan being repayable in full at the end of 20 years. The other proposal

is for a similar amount with an interest rate of 8·5 per cent. In this case, the loan would be repayable at the rate of £100 000 on the last day of the sixth and subsequent years. The balance would be repayable at the end of the twentieth year. The likely level of corporation tax is 50 per cent. The company uses a 10 per cent criterion rate in its investment appraisal.

Which alternative would you accept?

Model Solutions to the Problems

1. Discount rate for 10 per cent after 20 years=0·149
   ∴. present value of £16 000 receivable after 20 years=16 000×0·149=£2384
   On financial grounds alone the decisions should be not to purchase, since the outlay of £2500 secures an investment with a lower present value. There may be uncertainties, such as the health of the present beneficiary, which could lead to a different decision.

2. *Net Cash Investment* £9500

   Annual and Residual Cash Flows

Years	Annual Cash Flow	PV factor for 12%	Present Value
1 to 15	£1500	6·811	£10 216

   As the present value, using a 12 per cent rate, is greater than the net cash investment this project should be ranked with the other projects earning 12 per cent or more. For this purpose the profitability index would be 10 216/9500=1·08

3. *Net Cash Investment*

	Cost of machine	£15 000
	Installation and carriage	600
		15 600

   Annual and Residual Cash Flows

Year	Cost savings	Increase in tax	Capital allowances	Tax saved	Cash flow	PV factor for 10%	Present value
	£	£	£	£	£		£
1	3 000	—	9 360	4 680	7 680	0·909	6 981
2	5 000	1 500	1 560	780	4 280	0·826	3 535
3	5 000	2 500	1 170	585	3 085	0·751	2 317
4	5 000	2 500	877	439	2 939	0·683	2 006
5	5 000	2 500	658	329	2 829	0·621	1 757
6	—	2 500	—	—	(2 500)	0·564	(1 410)
	23 000	11 500	13 625	6 813	18 313		15 186
Residual value Nil			1 975	987	987	0·564	558
			15 600	7 800	19 300		15 744

   Since £15 744 is almost the same as the £15 600 investment, the rate of return is the criterion rate of 10 per cent.

159

4. *Net Cash Investment*

Cost of plant		110,000
Working capital:		
Year 1 15 000 × 0·909		13 635
Year 2 10 000 × 0·826		8 260
Marketing costs — Year 1		
10 000 × 0·909		9 090
Tax relief on above—Year 2		
5 000 × 0·826		(4 130)
Less		
Sale of existing plant	£2 000	
Less Balancing charge		
on £1 000 =	500	(1 500)
		£135 355

Annual and Residual Cash Flows

Year	Increase on profit	Tax	Capital allowances	Tax saved	Cash flow	PV factor for 10%	Present value
	£	£	£	£	£		£
1	10 000	—	110 000	55 000	65 000	0·909	59 085
2	25 000	5 000	—	—	20 000	0·826	16 520
3	25 000	12 500	—	—	12 500		
4	25 000	12 500	—	—	12 500		
5	25 000	12 500	—	—	12 500		
6	25 000	12 500	—	—	12 500	4·409 *	55 112
7	25 000	12 500	—	—	12 500		
8	25 000	12 500	—	—	12 500		
9	25 000	12 500	—	—	12 500		
10	25 000	12 500	—	—	12 500		
11	—	12 500	—	—	(12 500)	0·350	(4 375)
	235 000	117 500	110 000	55 000	172 500		126 342

Residual values

Working capital	£25 000						
Plant £5 000			(5 000)	(2 500)	27 500	0·350	9 625
			105 000	52 500	200 000		135 967

* PV factor for £1 for each of ten years 6·145
  less that for two years   1·736
                                      4·409

Rate of return is therefore just over 10 per cent.

5. *Net Cash investment*   £110 000
    (In this case the plant only)

Annual and residual cash flows

Year	Net rent	Addtl. tax	Capital allowances	Tax saved	Cash flow	PV factors for 10%	Present value
	£	£	£	£	£		£
1	14 000*	—	110 000	55 000	69 000	0·909	62 721
2	14 000	7 000	—	—	7 000		
3	14 000	7 000	—	—	7 000		
4	14 000	7 000	—	—	7 000		
5	14 000	7 000	—	—	7 000		
6	14 000	7 000	—	—	7 000	5·236	36 652
7	14 000	7 000	—	—	7 000		
8	14 000	7 000	—	—	7 000		
9	14 000	7 000	—	—	7 000		
10	14 000	7 000	—	—	7 000		
11	—	7 000	—	—	(7 000)	0·350	(2 450)
	140 000	70 000	110 000	55 000	125 000		96 923

Residual value:

Plant £5 000			(5 000)	(2 500)	2 500	0·350	875
			105 000	52 500	127 500		97 798

The leasing costs that would be saved through purchasing the machine do not have a present value greater than the cost of owning it, therefore the machine should be leased.

* Annual rental less saving of £1 000 ownership costs

6. ORIGINAL PROPOSAL

Net cash investment (using a 16% rate)

Plant costs	Year	−1	750 000 × 1·160 =	870 000
	Year	0	750 000 × 1·000 =	750 000
Grant receivable	Year	1	300 000 × 0·862 =	(258 600)
				1 361 400

Annual cash flow:
£300 000 per year for nine years 300 000 × 4·607 =   1 382 100

Therefore, the rate of return is just over *16 per cent*

AMENDED PROPOSAL

Net cash investment (using 14% rate)

Plant costs	Year	−1	950 000 × 1·140 =	1 083 000
	Year	0	950 000 × 1·000 =	950 000
Grant receivable	Year	1	400 000 × 0·877 =	(340 800)
				1 692 200

Annual cash flows:
£350 000 per year for nine years 350 000 × 4·946 =   1 731 100

Therefore, the rate of return is just over *14 per cent*. Both of these rates are in excess of the 12 per cent offered by other opportunities and would be acceptable on those grounds. It is instructive, however, to look at the return on the incremental investment in the latter example.

161

Incremental Investment
Additional investment in the amended proposal:

			(using 7% rate)	PV
Year	−1	200 000 × 1·070		214 000
Year	0	200 000 × 1·000		200 000
Year	1	(100 000) × 0·935		(93 500)
				320 500

Additional annual cash flows:
50 000 × 6·515 =   325 750

Therefore, the incremental investment has a rate of return of only 7 per cent, and the original proposals should be accepted and the incremental investment used for some other project earning 12 per cent or more.

EFFECT OF REDUCING ANNUAL CASH FLOWS BY £80 000 PER YEAR
ORIGINAL PROPOSAL

Net cash investment   (using 9% rate)

Year	−1	750 000 × 1·090	817 500
Year	0	750 000 × 1·000	750 000
Year	1	300 000 × 0·917	(275 100)
			1 292 400

Annual cash flows
£220 000 × 5·995 =   1 318 900

Therefore, the rate of return is reduced to just over 9 per cent and the project would be discarded in favour of others yielding 12 per cent.

AMENDED PROPOSAL

Net cash investment

Year	−1	950 000 × 1·090 =	1 035 500
Year	0	950 000 × 1·000 =	950 000
Year	1	400 000 × 0·917 =	(366 800)
			1 618 700

Annual cash flows
270 000 × 5·995 =   1 618 650

Therefore, the rate of return on the amended project would also fall to 9 per cent and the same criteria would apply. Since both forms of the project have a similar rate of return, then the rate of return on the incremental investment must also be of the order of 9 per cent.

7. Total present value of 8·75% loan
   Annual interest   £175 000
   Less tax relief at 50% 87 500
   Net cost   87 500
   Present value   87 500 × 8·514 =   744 975
   Repayment in 20 years time
   £2·0 million × 0·0149 =   298 000
                        1 042 975

Total present value of 8·5per cent loan. 10 %

Year	Interest	Less tax	Net interest	Loan repayt.	Total cash flow	PV factors	Present value
1	170 000	85 000	85 000	—	85 000 ⎫		
2	170 000	85 000	85 000	—	85 000 ⎪		
3	170 000	85 000	85 000	—	85 000 ⎬ 3·791		322 235
4	170 000	85 000	85 000	—	85 000 ⎪		
5	170 000	85 000	85 000	—	85 000 ⎭		
6	170 000	85 000	85 000	100 000	185 000	0·564	104 340
7	161 500	80 750	80 750	100 000	180 750	0·513	92 725
8	153 000	76 500	76 500	100 000	176 500	0·467	82 425
9	144 500	72 250	72 250	100 000	172 250	0·424	73 034
10	136 000	68 000	68 000	100 000	168 000	0·386	64 848
11	127 500	63 750	63 750	100 000	163 750	0·350	57 313
12	119 000	59 500	59 500	100 000	159 500	0·319	50 880
13	110 500	55 250	55 250	100 000	155 250	0·290	45 023
14	102 000	51 000	51 000	100 000	151 000	0·263	39 713
15	93 500	46 750	46 750	100 000	146 750	0·239	35 073
16	85 000	42 500	42 500	100 000	142 500	0·218	31 065
17	76 500	38 250	38 250	100 000	138 250	0·198	27 374
18	68 000	34 000	34 000	100 000	134 000	0·180	24 120
19	59 500	29 750	29 750	100 000	129 750	0·164	21 279
20	51 000	25 500	25 500	600 000	625 500	0·149	93 200
	2 507 500	1 253 750	1 253 750	2 000 000	3 253 750		1 164 647

The 8·75 per cent loan has the least cost in present value terms and should therefore be the one that is accepted.

1164294

Index

Made and printed in Great Britain by Clarke, Doble & Brendon Ltd, Plymouth and London